Living before God

Gracious God,
We are before you.
We are always before you.

You see us as we are and
Love us for ourselves.
You hear the words
We cannot say.
You know the longing
We cannot express.

Grant that it be enough for us
To be seen,
To be known, and
To be loved by you this moment.
AMEN.

LIVING *before* GOD

DEEPENING OUR SENSE
OF THE DIVINE PRESENCE

Ben Campbell Johnson

WILLIAM B. EERDMANS PUBLISHING COMPANY
GRAND RAPIDS, MICHIGAN / CAMBRIDGE, U.K.

Published by Wm. B. Eerdmans Publishing Co.
2140 Oak Industrial Drive N.E., Grand Rapids, Michigan 49505 /
P.O. Box 163, Cambridge CB3 9PU U.K.

Printed in the United States of America

05 04 03 02 01 00   7 6 5 4 3 2 1

Library of Congress Cataloging-in-Publication Data

Johnson, Ben Campbell.
Living before God: contemplative postures / Ben Campbell Johnson.
p.   cm.
ISBN 978-0-8028-4652-5 (pbk.: alk. paper)
1. Spiritual life — Christianity.   I. Title.
BV4501.2.J5385 2000
248.4 — dc21
99-049159

The author and publisher gratefully acknowledge permission to quote material from the following publications:

The lyrics of the hymn "When from Bondage," written by Delores Dufner, O.S.B., copyright © 1984, 1988, 1996 by the Sisters of the Order of St. Benedict, 104 Chapel Lane, St. Joseph, Minnesota 56374.

Excerpt from *The Song of the Bird* by Anthony de Mello. Copyright © 1982 by Anthony de Mello, S.J. Used by permission of Doubleday, a division of Random House, Inc.

Excerpts from *The God Who Comes* by Carlo Carretto. Copyright © 1974 by Carlo Carretto. Used by permission of Orbis Books, Claretian Publications, and Città Nuova.

Unless otherwise noted, the Scripture quotations in this publication are taken from the New Revised Standard Version of the Bible, copyright © 1989 by the Division of Christian Education of the National Council of Churches of Christ in the U.S.A., and used by permission.

To
Julie Johnson,
a saint in the making!

Contents

Introduction

"Living before God" defines one of the inescapable realities of our being in this world. We have no choice about the fact of "being before God," only about how we posture ourselves in God's presence. Some persons seem to live most of their lives without ever noticing the One who is their most attentive audience. Others attend God on occasion. Most of us need help in learning to live this great adventure. Along the way many have helped me, and I have written this book to share with you and others some of the things I have learned.

Many of God's saints have inspired my interest in living moment by moment in the presence of God. One of my first inspirations was Brother Lawrence in the monastery kitchen with his pots and pans, who was as prayerful there as when he received the Blessed Sacrament. A subsequent inspiration was Frank Laubach sitting on Signal Hill, letting God speak through his lips, and the inspiration I received from his writings. Much later, Jean-Pierre de Caussade came into my life, reveling in "the sacrament of the present moment." Saint Teresa of Ávila made her impression on me as she explored "the interior castle," from the outer courts to the center where His Majesty dwells. St. John of the Cross also helped me, as much as I could understand him, with his journey through the "dark night of the soul" to union with God. In my later years, Carlo Carretto, who testifies to knowing the divine presence in himself twenty-four hours out of twenty-four, has modeled for me a life of patient waiting before God. All these have helped me, but many others who will never be known to the masses have entered into my life, given me instruction, offered a word of encouragement, and then passed on. For all these emissaries of God, I am eternally grateful.

Through the years, these servants of God have helped me find various ways — you might call them postures — of being before God. These postures range from wondering about the divine mystery to acknowledging the presence of God in me, in my heart. These various stances have enabled me to become conscious of the divine presence and to respond to it. None of these can be called techniques that guarantee the divine presence, so I have called them postures, ways of being before God.

I have written this book for the seeking person who desires to know God, to live before God in a way that honors God's will. At the end of each chapter I have included several questions. Individual readers can reflect on these; readers in groups can use them for discussion, to aid their spiritual growth in community. I have included journaling exercises too. These will benefit individual readers and serve as enriching preparation for those gathering in small groups for prayer and sharing.

If you have had no previous experience of keeping a journal of your spiritual life, I hope you will begin to do so. I think you will find it beneficial. You may use a computer for your journaling or simply write down your thoughts in a small notebook. Record your responses to the suggestions I have made in the journaling exercises and notice what you discover. Mentally responding to my comments and questions will not be the same as putting your thoughts in writing. In the text itself I have also offered a variety of ways for you to use writing to deepen your sense of God's presence.

Thanks to Nan, my wife, to students who allowed me to talk with them about these ideas, to those who have influenced my life, and to all the companions I walk with on the pathway.

BEN CAMPBELL JOHNSON

CHAPTER ONE

Waking Up to God and to Life

I think there is nothing more tragic than to be asleep when you should be awake. Perhaps nothing more embarrassing, either.

Have you ever discovered in the midst of an exam that you had been asleep when one of the questions was discussed in class?

Do you recall awakening to a missed appointment?

Have you ever slept through a concert, an airplane departure, or an important interview?

I have. Bewildering, isn't it?

This loss of consciousness has happened to all of us. I remember a humiliating experience on one of my first trips to Chicago. I bought tickets to *Barefoot in the Park,* made my way back to the hotel, and decided to lie down for a few minutes before getting dressed for the play. It was one of those cold, snowy, windy days in Chicago. I had gotten chilled to the bone waiting in line for the tickets. The room was warm in contrast to the chilly weather outside. All the circumstances invited a relaxed sleep. When I awoke, it was 10:30 p.m. The play was over, and I was the proud holder of worthless tickets. Maybe this unplanned nap was not tragic in the larger scheme of things, but it was upsetting nevertheless.

During my second year in seminary, my wife and I lived in an apartment heated by a coal-burning stove. Since we had a new baby in the house, I fired up the old stove one evening and set the damper to burn all night. At one A.M. I awoke with the bedroom full of smoke. The apartment was in flames. I had just enough time to get my wife, the baby, and most of her clothes out of the building. The fire demolished all of our belongings, except for what we could grab on the way out of the flaming inferno. Losing virtually everything we owned was difficult, but sleeping through the fire would have been tragic for my young family and me.

Experiences like these leave us feeling stupid, undisciplined, or thoughtless of others, but another kind of sleep may be more tragic: life-sleep. Life-sleep is a quiescence in which persons seem to be awake — they open their eyes, get out of bed, eat breakfast, drive to work, go through the motions of the day — but they are not fully awake. In fact, they take on the tasks of the day unaware of a larger and more important dimension of life.

Many of these humanoids have no awareness of the purpose of their lives; they never have been opened to their depth, much less explored it; they possess only a faint awareness of the mystery that surrounds them. Missing out on these peculiarly human aspects of life leaves them deeply impoverished and restless.

Haven't you known some people like this? I have friends that seem to fall into this category. One has become rich but doesn't know what to do with his material security and success. Another is outwardly religious — attends church, gives money, acts pious — but doesn't seem to be aware of the depth out of which religious faith is born. And still another friend seems stuck in a mire of resentment and fear that stifles her creativity and impairs her imagination.

These dozing persons, afflicted with life-sleep, sometimes seem uncomfortable with their disease; others even consciously ignore it. Yet a small contingency, on occasion, actually tries to awaken. Tragically, a number of life-sleepers, like the well-known Rip Van Winkle, wake up near the journey's end.

What would it take to cure our somnambulism?

What would happen to us if we woke up?

The "Life-Sleep" Disease

"Life-sleep" describes a peculiar state of existence in which persons function effectively in the external world with little, if any, awareness of either the depth of the world or their own personal depth. Most who sleep through life don't even suspect, much less discover, what lies beneath the surface. Some even fail to wonder about the meaning of things. But most people, in my opinion, long to awaken to a fulfillment that has eluded them but can't find the way into this mysterious depth.

Those who live on the surface of things talk only about the trivial or mundane aspects of life. Perhaps we need not go so far to find "life-sleepers." Don't you recall times in your own life when the tasks of the day or the immediate responsibilities of family or work crowded out the more substantive aspects of your life?

Maybe the regular act of nightly sleep itself provides a metaphor of "life-sleep." What does it mean to go to sleep? For most of us the ritual probably includes going home, eating supper, watching television, going to the bedroom, undressing, turning down the covers, getting into bed, stretching out, beginning to relax, becoming drowsy, losing contact with the physical world, and gradually falling into unconsciousness. Every night we enter into that strange world of unconsciousness where dreams may occur, images may appear, and insights may come, but we have no power to determine these nighttime dramas. Everything occurs outside the bounds of our rational, free participation. This is precisely the meaning of life-sleep: things happen in a spiritual dimension outside of our conscious participation.

But life-sleep or wakeful sleep essentially operates in reverse. We awaken, arise, and perform our morning rituals in an unconscious manner that sets the tone for the day. Our habits of awaking, dressing, going to work, conducting business, and living through the day are carried out without our being aware of what we are really seeing, hearing, and feeling. When we live this way, we miss the spiritual depth of life. To awaken to this depth might be a great shock to our spiritual nature. Are we so well-rehearsed in sleeping through life that we wouldn't know what to do if we woke up?

Be forewarned. Just as the material world rests secure while we sleep through the night, so the spiritual world also remains actual and secure beneath our every step. It presents us with invitations and opportunities throughout our waking day, whether we attend them or not. This deeper dimension of existence surrounds us like the air, beckons us with persistent invitations, and seeks to show itself in subtle but recognizable ways. The reality of the spiritual aspects of life does not depend upon us but upon Another who cares more for us than we dare believe. The deciding factor does not rest with this Other but with us: this One acts and invites, but our participation depends upon our attending the presence that beckons us.

3

Some who have attended the deeper dimensions of life seem strange indeed to rational, one-dimensional souls. Imagine the experience of the wise men, who came all the way from Iran seeking the place Jesus was born. They traveled across the country, following a star. Imagine how they might have answered questions like "Where are you from?" and "Where are you going?" and "Who is your guide?" To the last question they would have answered, "A star." All of the "why" questions would have been terribly embarrassing to them. Something of an odd group, wouldn't you say? Others had not noticed the star, but they had, and followed it.

I suppose many persons considered Carlo Carretto, who also followed a star, a strange character. For twenty years in Italy, he had led a renewal movement of youth in affirming the faith and resisting Communism. At the age of forty-four, Brother Carlo left the security of the group, gave up his vocation of leadership, and took a ship to North Africa in answer to a call from God. Again and again he had to comfort his friends and especially his sister with the assurance that he was doing the right thing. He wrote to his sister, "Don't worry, Dolce, it's God who's calling me. I know His voice. Think of my life up till now: I've always followed the right star, haven't I?"[1] Carlo spent the next ten years in the North African desert, learning to pray.

Carlo attended the invitation of the Spirit. But his going to North Africa in obedience to a voice speaking from within challenges our commitment.

Life-Sleep in Biblical Imagery

Both Jesus and Paul invite disciples to wake up from life-sleep. In the records about Jesus' life and teaching, we discover that he dealt with this malady even in his own followers. Here is the story:

> Now the disciples had forgotten to bring any bread; and they had only one loaf with them in the boat. And he cautioned them, saying, "Watch out — beware of the yeast of the Pharisees and the yeast of Herod." They said to one another, "It is because we have no bread."
>
> And becoming aware of it, Jesus said to them, "Why are you talking about having no bread? Do you still not perceive or understand? Are

1. Carlo Carretto, *Letters to Dolcidia* (Maryknoll, N.Y.: Orbis Books, 1991), p. 19.

your hearts hardened? Do you have eyes, and fail to see? Do you have ears, and fail to hear? And do you not remember? When I broke the five loaves for the five thousand, how many baskets full of broken pieces did you collect?" They said to him, "Twelve." "And the seven for the four thousand, how many baskets full of broken pieces did you collect?" And they said to him, "Seven." Then he said to them, "Do you not yet understand?" (Mark 8:14-21)

When Jesus cautioned, "Watch out — beware of the yeast of the Pharisees and the yeast of Herod," he compared their influence to yeast. The literal-minded disciples did not understand that he meant the teaching of the Pharisees and the political power of Herod. They thought he was angry because they had brought no bread for the journey.

Jesus asked penetrating questions of these life-sleepers. "Do you still not perceive? Do you not remember? Do you have ears, and fail to hear? Do you have eyes, and fail to see?" All these questions not only challenged the disciples of Jesus but also challenge life-sleepers today, who know about the material aspects of life but do not know the spiritual depths of their own experience. Jesus' questions both affirm and invite. They affirm the reality of a deeper dimension in life, and they invite the sleepers into an awareness of it.

Jesus himself lived with a keen awareness of this dimension of the created world. He did see. He did hear. He did understand where the hidden God was at work. But the disciples' spiritual faculties of perception and understanding had been blunted.

Jesus had fed the five thousand with bread and fish. But for some reason the disciples had not grasped the mystery. In this miracle the Transcendent had broken into time; the Divine had presented itself to them. They should have known that Jesus was unconcerned about bread when he could feed the multitudes with a few loaves and fishes. Yet, they did not remember; they were blind, deaf, and clueless.

Perhaps he still asks those same questions of his followers: Do you still not perceive? Do you not understand? Are your hearts (emotions, awareness, and sensitivity) callused so that you do not feel anymore? Do you have eyes and fail to see? Ears and fail to hear? A mind and fail to remember what I do? You have the faculties to engage the deeper dimension of existence, but you are not using them.

How close does a miracle have to be for us to see it? How shocking must it be for us to appreciate it?

5

On another occasion at the end of Jesus' teaching, his disciples asked why he taught in parables. He explained that he used parables because those who saw did not perceive and those who heard did not understand. They fulfilled the prophecy of Isaiah: "You will indeed listen, but never understand, and you will indeed look, but never perceive" (Matt. 13:14).

Like the disciples, the multitudes that followed Jesus did not see. They, too, were life-sleepers. So Jesus taught them in parables, short stories that had the power to subvert their everyday world. By using these stories, Jesus turned their everyday world upside down. He opened their eyes and ears, and he sharpened their understanding so they could see the world in all its completeness.

One parable illustrates the point: "With what can we compare the kingdom of God, or what parable will we use for it?"

> It is like a mustard seed, which, when sown upon the ground, is the smallest of all the seeds on earth; yet when it is sown it grows up and becomes the greatest of all shrubs, and puts forth large branches, so that the birds of the air can make nests in its shade. (Mark 4:31-32)

When Jesus chose the mustard seed, the smallest of herbs, he cut deep into the value structure of his cultural world. In his mid-Eastern culture, size and proportion were measures of greatness. If a man was rich, he built a big house, he gave huge dinner parties with numerous guests, and he wore the finest clothes. But Jesus says the Kingdom of God consists of smallness, of things that seem to be of little value. And the growth, development, and expansion depend upon God. Perhaps his listeners' preoccupation with "bigness" blinded them to the Kingdom — an insight not alien to our own situation.

The mustard-seed metaphor points to a dimension of reality that seems small but grows and becomes enormous. The Parable of the Mustard Seed holds the cure for life-sleep. Still, both Jesus' followers and the religious professionals of his day took his sayings so literally that even his shocktherapy did not clear their vision or awaken their imagination. They heard Jesus' words but remained confused about the meaning. They were like the woman who attended the horticulturist's lecture on gardening. He said that mature horse manure was best for the garden. The woman in the audience raised her hand and asked, "How old should the horse be?"

Saint Paul invites the same kind of awakening when he says, "For

6

once you were darkness, but now in the Lord you are light. Live as children of light — for the fruit of the light is found in all that is good and right and true. . . . Therefore it [Scripture] says, 'Sleeper, awake! Rise from the dead, and Christ will shine on you'" (Eph. 5:8-9, 14).

Christ, the light of the world, shines upon the minds of persons, and as his light illuminates their understanding, it spills over into their lives. They live as persons of light, persons with meaning, with a sense of direction and purpose. This way of life produces goodness in them, right choices and actions; they live in harmony with God's intention. No wonder the apostle cries out, "Sleeper, awake! Rise from the dead, and Christ will shine on you."

In spite of the teaching of Jesus and the words of the Apostle Paul, many of us are still living blind to the real world. It is like living under the spell of a sorcerer, walking through life with our eyes closed to the mystery at work. We do not recognize what is being presented to us with every new day, and thus like actors with a single script we perform our memorized rituals on the stages of our lives. We live as though some mysterious force has flattened the world of an ordinary day, making it dull and uninteresting. What magician has waved his enchanted cloth and told us what to see? What prankster has bewitched us into believing that what we see is all there is?

What Does It Mean to Wake Up?

To be awake means to have our eyes opened so that we see, to have our ears opened so that we hear, to have our reason alert so that we understand. This is the biblical way of speaking of spiritual awareness. To be awake is the opposite of being asleep, deaf, and without understanding. Those anesthetized by earthly engagements and attachments must be shocked into wakefulness! For a moment this inner explosion disorients them and breaks their ordered way of thinking and perceiving. In that transitional moment, they glimpse the deeper dimension of reality!

Jesus provided this kind of disorienting shock by the things he did. His miracles stunned people so that many of them said, "We've never seen anything like this before." Such a shock caused his audience to wonder in amazement.

His parables had the same effect. "The Kingdom of heaven is like yeast that a woman took and mixed in with three measures of flour," he said (Matt. 13:33). His listeners were compelled to wonder what he meant by yeast and flour, and what significance these common kitchen supplies could possibly hold.

But Jesus' healings were themselves paradigmatic. When he healed a blind man, he demonstrated how "unseeing" persons could be made to see by his touch. When he healed the paralytic, he showed that unfeeling persons could be made to feel and engage unexplored dimensions of their psyche. And when he unstopped deaf ears, he revealed how spiritually deaf persons could be made to hear. Each of these healings dramatized the recovery of a capacity lost by neglect or fearful rejection.

It is possible, I believe, to wake up, to become aware. Awakening occurs in many ways. Some open their eyes with a start because of a noise or a touch, others with a jolt because of a shocking experience. Some slowly and gradually come to the consciousness of a new day.

No matter how deeply I reflect on a human being waking up to the vast reaches of the spiritual dimensions, I always conclude its occurrence is a mystery. Even awakening from sleep is mysterious. I don't fully understand how one emerges from the deep silence of sleep, becomes aware, and arises to a new day. From the first twitch of the sleeper on the pillow to the fully dressed human walking out the door — when you think about it, it's something of a wonder.

This daily experience of waking up does indeed provide a metaphor of a spiritual awakening, a waking up to life's depth. You might be awakened by some slight change in your body position, or by an alarm going off. Or you might come to the end of your rest and slowly become conscious. Perhaps you are roused by a small, conscious thought that you have. Then you turn over and rest a little more. Next you sit up. You open your eyes to discover that the world is still there, the same one you left several hours earlier in the dark. Now it is light, but your eyes haven't adjusted to the light, so you squint. Then slowly you stand and stretch. You think about where you are and what you'll do first today. You then take the first step into a new day.

You reach for your bedroom slippers and put them on, along with a robe. You make your way downstairs to the kitchen, turn on the lights, pull out the coffee, and make a pot for you and a pot for her. While the coffee brews, you go outside and pick up the daily paper, pull off the wrapper, and come back to the kitchen. By this time, one cup has brewed, and you pour it and sit down with the paper. You have performed the first ritual of the day; you have begun a new day.

In a similar way we can talk about the things that happen when a person is spiritually awakened. Most life-sleepers rest comfortably in a mode of life inherited from their primary, social world. This world has given them their language, their set of values, their role models, their ways of relating, and their sense of identity and worth. But sometimes something happens to a life-sleeper — she has an unsatisfied hunger or an unanswered question or experiences pain. The occurrence causes her to wake up, jolts her out of her sleep just like an alarm going off in the morning. Perhaps this is the first time she has become aware of pain, like the pain you can get in your shoulder from sleeping in the wrong position during the night. The awakening may occur because of a persistent question that feeds the yearning for God. The pain and the question combine to shake up the order in her life. Through the mystery of goodness and love, she begins to wonder about her life. She may ask who she really is or how to create secure relationships. These little experiences of pain, fear, doubt, questioning, and wondering create openings just wide enough for the light to shine into her consciousness. These shocking experiences are the equivalent of drawn shades being opened to let in the daylight. As the light shines, even faintly, the darkness begins to be dispelled.

We can describe a process of spiritual awakening, but we cannot dissolve the mystery. Seeing with the eyes of the heart and feeling the transformation that follows create a new perspective on life, but none can fully explain how or why it happens.

Ways of Awakening

When we survey the experiences of persons who have been awakened to reality, we see that the awakening can be triggered in a variety of ways. Sometimes a life-sleeper is awakened by a question like "Did you ever stop to think what you're doing with your life?" Sometimes just stopping to think is enough to awaken a soul. Those who resist being awakened say, "I dare not stop to think, because if I did, I wouldn't know how to get started again."

Sacred encounters have a way of shocking our consciousness that undermines old ways of thinking. Our encounter with the Holy may be like that of Isaiah in the temple. It may be like that of Paul on the road to Damascus. It may be like that of the blind man who, at Jesus' first touch, saw men as trees walking, but then, at Jesus' second touch, saw clearly. Or we may suddenly see the depth in life in the routine experience of a worship service. A young woman in one of my classes described an experience in church when the presence of Christ became personally real to her. Though she had been baptized as a baby and had attended church all of her life, it was not until she was seventeen that she awakened from life-sleep.

Some persons have been awakened by a powerful vision of what their life is meant to be. This sort of vision came to Peter on the rooftop in Joppa. The images and the voice that spoke to him introduced him to a new way of looking at Gentiles. Peter didn't create this vision; it was given to him. The message contradicted everything he had been taught. His most trusted authority was challenged and annulled. His vision had the same effect as Jesus' touching of the blind man's eyes — his eyes were opened, and he went away seeing, too.

An applicant to our doctoral program wrote about her reasons for desiring the degree. She had had a vision of wading through a swamp until she came to a clearing where there seemed to be a building like a church. Suddenly people began coming out of the forest, all kinds of people — small, large, black, white, poor, rich. She heard a voice speaking to her: "Go rebuild my church." This commission seemed too great for her to undertake. Then an angel appeared who seemed larger than life. He stood next to the church, and it became clear to her that only with God's assistance could she help to rebuild the church. The vision propelled her into action.

A positive urge that results in a new form of behavior may awaken our spirit. A Samaritan is walking down the road. When he sees a Jew lying in the ditch, he walks over and, out of compassion, ministers to him. This action contradicts the Samaritan's whole cultural upbringing, but he does it anyway. Similar things happen when a salesman discovers that customers are not things to be used but persons to serve. The world forever changes for him. I knew a woman whose life was changed because she saw a play about street people; afterwards she went home to found a ministry to the homeless.

Sometimes the pain of conscience awakens people. The realization of wrongness, of having failed, of having contradicted one's vision and values creates such disappointment that a person cannot live with herself. A woman vows to be faithful to her husband, but tensions arise, affections are tested, resolve for the moment relaxes, and she finds herself with another man. Feelings of remorse drive her to seek counsel and forgiveness, and these twin experiences of failure and forgiveness introduce her to the dimension of spirit.

10

Some are awakened when their life experience begins to unsettle their inherited worldview. The world they inherited had no depth, no sense of mystery, but their life experience includes mysterious encounters with the Beyond, coincidences that defy explanation, and yearnings that cannot be fulfilled in a flat world. The sense of Another in their midst, a feeling of presence and power in a moment of weakness or helplessness, and the old life posture strains under the pressure. These persons begin to feel like a grown man in a kid's trousers — the soul outgrows its clothing.

Once our eyes have been opened, we can never again go back to our original innocence. Once we have seen, we cannot "unsee" — the world has depth! As someone has said, "You can't un-ring a bell!"

The process of awakening has no end. Some have believed that once they awakened, they were permanently aware. Not true. We continue to awaken more and more deeply throughout our life journey.

Questions for Reflection and Discussion

1. How do the "asleep" and "awake" metaphors apply to the spiritual life?

2. What do Jesus' words about wakefulness mean?

3. When have you been awakened in your life? What did it mean to you? How did you respond to the awakening? What are the consequences of it in your life?

Journaling Exercises

1. Recall a time when you awakened to the presence of God in your life. When did it occur? What was it like for you?

2. In two or three paragraphs, complete this sentence: "At present my life with God is . . ."

3. Write a memo to God expressing your gratitude for an experience of awakening.

CHAPTER TWO

Wondering about the Mystery

Can you recall a time in your life that you were utterly amazed? Haven't there been moments when you were awed by the brilliance of a sunset or a full moon, when a power from within gripped you with wonderment? Haven't astonishing things happened in your life, like meeting someone unexpectedly, someone whom you had thought of just minutes before? What are we to make of these occurrences which seem to come spontaneously and which gently shake us into awareness that life is more than a flat, predictable cycle without variance or surprise? I believe there is something inherent in the created order, in the unfolding of our lives, and in all our compelling searches for meaning and fulfillment that points to a mysterious presence that surrounds and engulfs our lives.

While the mystery may break into our consciousness in unpredictable moments and for only brief times, I believe we are, nevertheless, surrounded by mystery. Like a thick fog, it encircles us, grasps us, and on occasion invites us into its embrace. Often, when we are not even remotely considering this mystery, a giant hand reaches out and touches us briefly with wonder or amazement, only to be quickly withdrawn and hidden again in the clouds that cloak us. But, when the immediate experience passes, we are left with the memory of the hand and the wonder it evoked. Where did this hand come from? Why did it touch us with wonder? And why were we touched at this particular moment?

Sometimes I think we are like a fish in the sea that wonders where the ocean is. Imagine the little minnow swimming alongside its mother and asking, "Mother, where is the sea?" The mother answers, "You are in

13

it." But, unconvinced, the little minnow swims off, looking for the sea. Is the mystery like that? We live in mystery, breathe mystery, yet we look past the mystery that surrounds us and even deny it. Still, the mystery continues, resisting our every effort to define, contain, or control it.

Whether or not you have thought much about it, I suspect you have encountered the mystery. You may not have marked the encounter as something special; perhaps you didn't even reflect on it. Nevertheless, it happened to you and left its mark. This state is not a posture so much as it is a condition. It is being pursued by Someone beyond you who desires to meet you. I recall an encounter with the mystery that left me with a sense that my life included more than I could define. The things that happen, I believe, are more than random events spun out by a wheel of fate. On occasion these special moments testify that Someone is aware of us and is sending secret, encoded messages which tantalize and entice us with wonder.

Such occurrences do not happen often enough to create patterns or provide us with enough information to break the code, but they do come frequently enough to alert us to the continuous presence of mystery. I recall quite vividly one such incident that happened to me.

I was driving home from a faculty meeting at which my colleagues had voted unanimously for me to become Professor of Christian Spirituality at Columbia Theological Seminary. The background to this decision began developing much earlier. Some ten years before, when I was fifty-five, I felt called to spend an extended time in solitude to discuss God's direction for my remaining years. I made arrangements to spend two weeks in a monastery, Christ in the Desert, which is about seventy miles from Sante Fe, New Mexico. I spent my time there wondering about how my final years of ministry should be invested. Time was too short to do something trivial and the work too important to be focused in the wrong direction. My deep intuition told me that I should focus on Christian spirituality and lead both clergy and laypersons in discovering and living before God.

The amazing thing about the faculty vote stemmed from conversations I had had with a blue-ribbon committee of the faculty during the fall semester. After I had met with this influential committee about the issue of changing my faculty appointment from Professor of Church Growth to Professor of Christian Spirituality, the committee had concluded that the faculty would never vote for this change. Yet, here I was, driving home from a meeting in which the faculty had just voted unanimously for this change to occur! And as I drove along, the hand veiled in mystery reached out and touched me on the shoulder, and a voice said, "You didn't believe I could do that, did you?"

When I realized that the impossible had suddenly occurred, I was struck with wonder and amazement! It had happened! Someone who had spoken to me a decade before, telling me what direction my life should take, was now speaking again, assuring me that the events were no accident, no matter of chance or fate. And I was filled with wonder!

This sense of wonder momentarily shut down the rational faculties of my mind. In that moment I entered a dimension beyond reason and logic and control. The disclosure of the mystery in my consciousness so filled me with joy that all I could do was whisper words of praise and gratitude. The awareness did not last long, just long enough to mark my memory with a sense of the divine. The mystery that surrounds us had made a point, lest I should forget.

The Meaning of Wonder

Just what do we mean by wonder? "Wonder" is both a noun and a verb. And in the human psyche, wonder produces amazement, puzzlement, awe, fascination, and enchantment.

"Wonder" as a noun suggests an emotion aroused by something awe-inspiring, astounding, or marvelous. For me this awesome moment of wonder came because I had been part of a God-event in which the impossible had occurred. For others this deep sense of wonder comes when they have an encounter with nature. Listen to David Steindl-Rast's description of how an engagement with nature affected him:

> I walked out onto a dock in the Gulf of Mexico. I ceased to exist. I experienced being a part of the sea breeze; the movement of the water and the fish, the light rays cast by the sun, the colors of the palms and tropical flowers. I had no sense of past or future. It was not a particularly blissful experience: it was terrifying. It was the kind of ecstatic experience I'd invested a lot of energy in avoiding. I did not experience myself as the same as the water, the wind, and the light, but as participating with them in the same system of movement. We were all dancing together.[1]

1. David Steindl-Rast, *Gratefulness, the Heart of Prayer: An Approach to Life in Fullness* (New York: Paulist Press, 1984), p. 23.

Sometimes wonder is evoked by an event inexplicable by the laws of nature, an event some would call a miracle. How can you explain meeting someone at an unexpected time and place and the mysterious impact their presence has upon you?

I first met Eddie at a conference in Chicago. He was pastor of a growing church, a man with a bright smile and a radiant countenance, the kind of glow that warms the heart. Later that year Eddie became a Thompson scholar and studied with us at Columbia Seminary for ten days. When funds became available for pilgrimages for pastors, I invited Eddie to make a pilgrimage to the Holy Land with me.

We began a daylong retreat at the little church on top of the Mount of Beatitudes. As he was leaving the church, Eddie saw a man who had been his mentor for a long time. He had just been thanking God for this man and praying for him while on his knees in the chapel. And then Eddie walked out of the church to meet the man who had been his role model throughout high school, his sponsor at Loyola University, and a participant in his ordination to ministry. A special man. He ran up to this old friend and hugged him.

Eddie felt the wonder of praying for this man and walking into his arms immediately afterward. Of course, all of us on the outside of this event can explain it. We can give a rational account of the sequence of events that led to this moment. But logic and reason did not dominate Eddie's emotions. He had knelt, prayed, and left the church only to meet the man he had prayed for just seconds before. For him it was no accident, and reason could not dispel the wonder of the experience.

Sometimes wonder takes the form of a feeling of puzzlement or doubt. When Jesus appeared to a group of his disciples after his crucifixion, he received a mixed response. Scripture states that Jesus commanded his disciples to meet him in Galilee after the resurrection. A group of his followers gathered in Galilee, and they saw the risen Christ. And "when they saw him, they worshiped him; *but some doubted*" (Matt. 28:17; my italics). Amazement and doubt often occur together, and we see this in Jesus' disciples. When these followers of Jesus went to Galilee to meet him, his risen presence evoked wonder in some and doubt in others. They wondered because they could not explain his escape from the tomb and his traverse from Jerusalem to Galilee; they doubted because dead people don't normally come back to life.

Wonder or amazement also describes a state of being. My experience of driving home from the faculty meeting and being filled with wonder was such a state. The kinds of experiences I have described — mine, Steindl-Rast's, Eddie's, and the disciples' — for a moment paralyze reason and drive it into ecstasy, and then another dimension of reality breaks into consciousness. No one controlled these occurrences; they came about spontaneously. But they made persons know they had brushed up against the mystery.

A Biblical View of Wonder

Wonder in the life and teaching of Jesus often seems to be described as "amazement." Jesus experienced amazement at the unbelief of his followers (Mark 6:6). But he was also amazed at the faith of Gentiles who came to him (Matt. 8:10). Frequently his words and actions produced amazement in the crowds who listened to him (Matt. 15:31; Mark 1:27). Wonderment was the experience of the people around Jesus who saw or heard things that did not make sense. These things Jesus was doing did not fit their worldview, nor did they conform to their expectations. They were amazed. When events challenge our way of seeing, amazement occurs and opens the door to faith and transformation. We may emerge from the state of wonder with an awareness of a deeper dimension of existence, or we may turn away from that invitation to believe and harden our resistance to the mystery. These various aspects of wonder come out in the account of Jesus' healing of the paralyzed man in Capernaum. Mark gives an account of this wonder-packed event:

> When he returned to Capernaum after some days, it was reported that he was at home. So many gathered around that there was no longer room for them, not even in front of the door; and he was speaking the word to them.
> Then some people came, bringing to him a paralyzed man, carried by four of them. And when they could not bring him to Jesus because of the crowd, they removed the roof above him; and after having dug through it, they let down the mat on which the paralytic lay. When Jesus saw their faith, he said to the paralytic, "Son, your sins are forgiven."
> Now some of the scribes were sitting there, questioning in their hearts, "Why does this fellow speak in this way? It is blasphemy! Who can forgive sins but God alone?" At once Jesus perceived in his spirit

17

that they were discussing these questions among themselves; and he said to them, "Why do you raise such questions in your hearts? Which is easier, to say to the paralytic, 'Your sins are forgiven,' or to say, 'Stand up and take your mat and walk'?

"But so that you may know that the Son of Man has authority on earth to forgive sins" — he said to the paralytic — "I say to you, stand up, take your mat and go to your home." And he stood up, and immediately took the mat and went out before all of them; so that they were all amazed and glorified God, saying, "We have never seen anything like this!" (Mark 2:1-12)

This healing event in Capernaum created amazement. Mark ends the story of Jesus healing the paralytic by saying, "They were all amazed and glorified God, saying, 'We have never seen anything like this!'" Something shocked them out of their normal way of seeing. They had an encounter with the mystery that left them without explanation. "We have never seen anything like this!" What is "this"? To what does "this" refer?

Could it mean that we have never seen anything like these four friends who have taken the paralyzed man to Jesus? That we have never seen such generosity, such risk, such an expenditure of energy to get him around the crowd and down through the roof into the presence of Jesus? Was this the source of amazement?

Or does "this" refer to the words and actions of Jesus? Jesus stopped speaking to the crowd gathered around him. He looked at the paralytic and said, "Son, your sins are forgiven." Were they amazed because they had never seen anyone who was so patient with an interruption or was so powerful in his speech? "Son, your sins are forgiven." Were they amazed that Jesus did what only God can do — forgive sins?

Could "this," the action that created the amazement, refer to the attitude of the scribes sitting in the room? They questioned in their hearts, "Why does this fellow speak in this way? . . . Who can forgive sins but God alone?" After seeing the graciousness of Jesus in speaking forgiveness to this man whom they had known since he was born, maybe the crowd was amazed that the scribes of the local synagogue were compelled to discount Jesus' actions.

Or does "this" refer to the power of Jesus not only to forgive this paralyzed man but to heal him as well? Perhaps "this" refers to Jesus' command: "Stand up, take your mat, and go to your home." Or maybe "this" refers to a paralyzed man brought in by four friends who now is walking away, carrying the mat upon which he has lain for years. Was the crowd amazed at the power of Jesus' command or the restored power of the paralytic?

Any one of these occurrences could have created wonder and amazement in the minds and hearts of the crowd, but combine them and the wonderment becomes overwhelming. The Bible is filled with encounters, actions, and occurrences that create wonder in people's hearts.

This is not the only incident in which we find Jesus creating wonder by his words and actions. Amazement also characterizes the response of those who followed him about from place to place. What are we to say about this man, Jesus, who created wonder? How was he related to the mystery?

Other accounts in the Bible describe the wonder not only of Jesus' actions but those of his followers, like Peter at Pentecost, Paul in the Philippi jail, and John on the Isle of Patmos. The accounts in the Newer Testament build upon the experiences of wonder in the Older Testament, like the call of Abraham, the sacrifice of Isaac, and the crossing of the Red Sea.

The list of events in the Bible that evoke wonder and amazement is practically endless:

A voice speaks,
A bush burns,
A sea parts,
A mountain quakes,
An ax-head floats,
An angel announces,
A body rises,
A spirit comes,
A sheet descends.

For Christians especially, the encounter with Jesus today has the power to evoke wonder. With us now as with those long ago, wonder is not a state induced by self-hypnosis but a spontaneous invasion of the mystery that grasps our consciousness in unexpected ways and in unpredictable moments. Wonder is not the result of rational reflection on events but the consequence of an openness and receptivity to an encounter with the living Christ who comes to us, touches us, speaks to us, and fills us with amazement!

When we read the story of Jesus, we often find ourselves

astounded by his birth (the annunciation)
amazed by his wisdom (Jesus in the temple)
puzzled by his teaching (the parables)
awed by his living presence (the resurrection and promised Spirit).

So, like his mother, Mary, we still have much to ponder in our hearts.

From Wonder to Wondering

Wonder is not limited to the Bible. Wonder awakened and drew the Israelites into a living relationship with the Holy, and it led the Greeks to the fountain of philosophy. Wonder still awakens modern persons to a depth within themselves that they had not known before. This wondering serves as an invitation to meaning.

And for persons who know something of the mystery, the experience of wonder nourishes the roots of religious knowing; but when we cease to wonder, the passion for God dries up, the energy for life evaporates, and spiritual joy and delight in God turn to boredom and routine. Perhaps we need to capture once again the role of wondering.

Do you remember that wonder is both a noun and a verb? My comments thus far have been about the noun, about something that happens to us when we encounter the mystery, a spontaneous, unexpected, powerful event. "Wonder" as a verb defines a practice that we can choose to engage in. For example, we can wonder about the mystery that surrounds us. I can wonder about the experience I had on my way home from the faculty meeting. So "wonder" as a verb is a "walking around," subjective word that describes an inquiring response to the things we see, feel, touch, and hear. This "walking around" word permits us to marvel at those things we see or experience, to muse over the things that have happened to us. "Wondering" describes us as seeking, questioning, searching beings who are trying to make sense of our experiences and milk their meanings.

I am suggesting that "wonder" (noun) invites "wonder" (verb). Wonder about the things that have happened to us, wonder about the mystery that surrounds us, wonder about the yearnings and hungers of the soul. Generally, the first question that a person awakened by wonder asks is "Why?" The "why's" of our lives begin a chain reaction that will

20

not let us rest until we find a solution to the reason for and the meaning of our being.

The question of meaning arises because the human spirit has been touched by mystery. Once the scales have dropped from our eyes, once we have had our eyes opened and discovered that the world has depth, we can never slip back into an innocent sleep.

Experiments in Wondering

I cannot imagine that you would have read this far without reviewing your life experiences for moments of wonder. You may have found a few attention-getters or temporary life-stoppers when tragedy struck, or some amazing revelation that came to you, but I suspect most of your experiences were simpler. Did your experiences of wonder leave you with questions you have never answered? The questions lie around the edges of our memory, overshadowed by the demands of the day. Since the answers to "why" or "how" are not pressing us nearly so hard as making a marriage work or rearing a child, we let them go. And we are the poorer for it.

When we ignore the hints of meaning in our lives for too long, we become victims of our own neglect. The pressure of the day robs us of time for reflection; the anesthetic of television and the pressure of too many appointments seal off our deeper selves, and we live complacently on the surface of life.

I am inviting you to see, to see in a new way, to forsake the old defenses you have used to escape from yourself. I urge you to pay attention to your life, to what has happened in the past and what is happening today. Look beneath the ordinary happenings, see into the meaning of these events, trust that the world is not flat, meaningless, and going nowhere. Wondering offers the pathway into this world of depth that at least exposes us to the mystery "in which we live and move and have our being."

To see with "new eyes," eyes that see the invisible, eyes that can gaze upon the wonders of being, you must be willing to let go of accustomed ways of seeing and view your life from a different perspective. If you have looked at the world as flat and your experiences as predictable, and if you have consciously or unconsciously ruled out everything that does not fit your paradigm, a new way of seeing may be very exciting and challenging for you.

A colleague of mine was teaching a group about new ways of seeing. Suddenly, he turned to the chalkboard, took a piece of chalk, and drew three rows of dots that formed a square like the one below. He asked each person in the class to connect all the dots with four straight lines without picking up their pens.

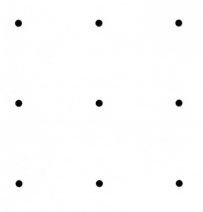

Hint: To perform the task, you have to get out of the box in the same way I am asking you to "get out of the box" and wonder. (See p. 26 for the answer.)

There are a number of things you may wonder about:

1. The longings that you feel

Your deep yearnings for fulfillment. Are you looking for fulfillment through a greater sense of community? Of purpose? Of value and meaning in your life?

2. The questions you can't help asking:

> Who am I?
> Where did I come from?
> What am I doing here?
> Where am I going?

22

3. Strange happenings

In addition to these yearnings and questions, you can probably look back over your life and discover inexplicable occurrences. To ease your anxiety or to escape some deeper, possibly threatening memory, you may have dismissed these occurrences as accidents or coincidences. But such happenings may not have been random occurrences at all. What if life is not "a tale told by an idiot, full of sound and fury, signifying nothing," and everything that has happened to you has been communicating a message to you?

4. Your recurring thoughts

Sometimes thoughts that come to you in a convincing manner will not leave you alone. Did you ever wonder where these thoughts come from?

5. The important people in your life

God speaks to us through people he sends into our lives. What does it feel like when you are being spoken to by God?

What do you discover when you wonder about each of these important aspects of your life? I surely cannot predict where these musings will take you, but wondering serves as a powerful agent of awakening again and again. So, beware!

Wonder, Wondering, and Wonderful

I have been endeavoring to explore the experience of wonder in a way that begins to open up the divine mystery. Looking at wonder as both a state and an act provides a twin approach. Over one kind of wonder (noun) we have no control; the other kind (verb) we can initiate and sustain. Hopefully, you have begun to reflect on the suggestions I've made and have also begun to wonder about your life.

Much of our life before God seems abstract, such as "mystery," "wonder," and "faith." Most of us struggle to grasp the profound meaning that lies behind these words and experiences. Most often I can "see" better when I have a model or story to lead me. Perhaps the experience of a new

friend of mine will offer this kind of help to you. I met Louise in an interesting way, and her wonder-filled story embodies an amazing transformation.

I met Louise while I was making one of my day-long retreats at the
Monastery of the Holy Spirit, a Trappist monastery near Conyers, Georgia. (For more than thirty years I have been making retreats at this monastery. Since my experience at Christ in the Desert, I have set aside a day
each month for the renewal of my life and vision.) On this particular day
I took a long walk to visit old friends in the area. As we talked, they told
me about Louise, a woman who once had worked for CNN and now
rented a house from them to be near the monastery. I felt an immediate
interest in meeting her. The next morning after mass, I went out to meet
her, but I didn't see her.

When I inquired of one of the women who had attached herself to
the monastery as an oblate, she told me that Louise, too, was an oblate
and that Father Gus, the retreat master, had her phone number. I got the
number and made an appointment to see her that afternoon.

I spent nearly three hours listening to her story of pain and awakening. Louise was an adopted child of Italian immigrants. They were from
nobility, but during the Depression the father gambled away their money,
and the whole family ended up on the street, destitute. A priest in upstate
New York allowed them to live in the basement of the rectory.

While Louise was still quite young, a visiting priest sexually mo-
lested her. When the abuse was discovered, she was sent away to boarding
school. Under the tutelage of the nuns and through their teaching and
positive modeling, she experienced her spiritual formation.

When she graduated, she offered herself to the convent, but since
she was an illegitimate child, they refused to admit her. This crushed her
spirit, and she left the church for fifteen years.

When she was about thirty-five, she began to wonder about the
pain and emptiness of her life. One day in her home she sat down to pray.
She began to speak aloud to God: "I want to know you and love you. I
don't know how to get along with your church, but I do want you in my
life." As she prayed, her burden of anger and resentment lifted, and she
felt free and on the way to new discoveries. She began to wonder what her
life was about and how to fulfill its intention.

Given her new sense of God, she was confronted with the necessity
of finding a church. After visiting one congregation, she told the priest
that she wanted to learn to pray. He put her in touch with a charismatic

prayer group that helped for a time but eventually did not provide quite the nurture she needed. When she went to the priest again, he sent her to the Monastery of the Holy Spirit, where she met Father Gus, who became her faithful spiritual director. For several years he has been talking with her and guiding her.

After two or three years she felt the urge to devote herself more fully to prayer and a life of complete obedience to Christ. She spoke repeatedly with Father Gus about resigning from her position in the media business, but he kept telling her to wait. Finally, he agreed with her plan.

She counted up her assets and discovered that by living frugally, she could get along very well. When she retired from CNN, she was making a handsome six-figure salary, but money and success did not satisfy her deeper needs. Her encounter with the mystery had reordered her values and had given her a taste of reality that meant more than her worldly success or her monetary rewards.

So she resigned from her job in order to devote her life to humble service and prayer. Soon after her resignation, her husband wanted to move to Canada, and she, being obedient and supportive, moved with him. She used this detour in her plans as a time for immense spiritual growth.

This wonderful woman, who now has such a deep sensitivity to God and a fullness of life she could not find in earthly success or earthly gains, embodies wonder, wondering, and wonderful. She is herself a wonder, an adopted child who was sexually abused, then shipped away from home and rejected by those who taught her about a loving God. How could she ever come to God? She filled her life with earthly achievement and its rewards as a substitute for God. But somehow these material acquisitions could not fill the deep, deep longing in her soul. A seed had been planted that refused to die.

One day the agonizing hunger became so great that she could no longer ignore it. The mystery invaded her consciousness in the form of hunger and longing. Acknowledging God and opening up her life drew her into the mystery and wonder of God.

Perhaps nothing less than the amazement of divine love could have erased the pain of her early rejection by the sisters and her anger at the church. But the wonder of unconditional love wiped out her bitterness and filled her with a deep attraction to God's very Self.

Her encounter with God created wonder in her life.

That wonder took many forms — returning to church, trusting a priest, praying with charismatics, seeking a spiritual director, and leaving her job for a religious vocation. I can almost hear her questions: "Where have you been, God? Why do you continue loving me? How can I get to know you?"

The wonder of her meeting God and her sustained wondering about God's presence in her life has led her to become a truly wonder-full person. In all my years of listening to people describing their life journeys, I have never heard a person so calm, so whole, so natural, who became that way in such a few brief years.

Questions for Reflection and Discussion

1. What is the meaning of "wonder" as a noun? As a verb? How is the noun form different from the verb form?

2. How is "wonder" the anteroom of faith?

3. Think about a particular moment of wonder in your life. How would you describe it?

Journaling Exercises

1. Review your life and make a list of the things that have created wonder in you.

2. In the form of a prayer, write about the things you wonder (verb) about in your life today. "Dear God, I wonder . . ."

3. Complete this sentence: "My life would be wonderful if (or, is wonderful because) . . ."

Answer to the puzzle:

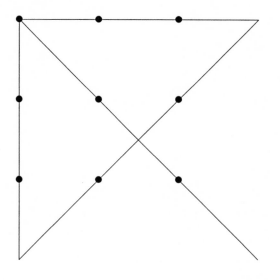

CHAPTER THREE

Engaging the Word

Wondering, a gift given to humans but withheld from other creatures, provides abundant energy and enthusiasm for searching for the mystery of God. Wondering presses against the boundaries of all that is known; wondering probes answers that no longer seem relevant; wondering edges close to the divine mystery; and wondering keeps us alert and alive to new possibilities. Perhaps no other human capacity ranks higher than wonder in our intention to live before God.

Wonder will not permit us to live complacent lives filled with ready-made answers. But wonder without information and discipline can often lead us astray; it requires substantive material for its task. In the words of Scripture we find material to nurture and inspire wonder.

Insights from Scripture

Perhaps the first contemplative posture should be sitting with bowed heads before the sacred scripture, the Holy Bible. The text of Scripture can be approached in a variety of ways. In fact, through the years there have been more ways of engaging Scripture than I can recount here. Some have read the Bible for history; others have read the Bible to discredit it because it did not concur with the latest scientific theories. Still others have read it through the eyes of a literary critic. And many have read the Bible as a magical book, seeking precise answers to personal questions simply by opening the pages at random and pointing to a verse. Not a few

Christians have read the Bible as a source of dogma, considering it a collection of frozen texts of truth.

I recognize and appreciate the work that scholars have done in interpreting Scripture. Their work is of the utmost importance. But there are ways to reach beyond these critical approaches and to read Scripture to enter into its truth, and thereby into the presence of God. It is the Word itself with which we deal, not words about the Word. Reading Scripture must not become an end in itself; it should lead us to God. We humans must deal primarily with God, before whom we live — not the Bible or doctrine.

For our method of encounter with the text of Scripture, we will examine one of the original ways that serious Christians engaged the text. To discover this approach, I have chosen to go back in time and look at the way early monks took in Scripture. Like us, they were interested not so much in formulating doctrine as in meeting the Word in the words, encountering the God of whom Scripture spoke. Gregory the Great, head of the church from 590 to 604 A.D., offers insight into the faith and practice of Christians with regard to Scripture that can be instructive to us.

Insights from Saint Gregory

Gregory the First was a reforming pope. He believed that we live before God in two ways — in the active life of service and works of compassion like teaching or feeding the hungry or reclaiming those who have wandered from God, and in the inner life of contemplation.

In the contemplative life, persons rested from the active works of service and compassion and gave themselves to prayer and the contemplation of God. Like many of the ancients, Gregory illustrated his idea of contemplation by pointing to the examples of Mary and Martha. Martha busied herself with the tasks of cooking and preparing the meal, while Mary sat at the feet of Jesus, conversing with and caring for him.

By dividing life into active engagement with the world and quiet engagement in the contemplation of God, Gregory was not suggesting that one must choose between compassion and contemplation. Rather, he was indicating that the life of a faithful person tended to emphasize one aspect more than the other. He was careful to encourage Christ's followers not to pull back from engagement with the neighbor. He urged them to serve their brothers and sisters when the signs indicated that they needed help. But he preferred a life of contemplative reflection, although he himself was constantly engaged with the church's earthly demands.

Most of us twentieth-century folk would not wish to make such a sharp division between the life of prayer and the life of service. I think Gregory's understanding of the faith reflects the theology and spiritual vision of the era. Like many of the early church fathers, Gregory believed in the sinfulness of human beings and the infinite, inexhaustible holiness of God, a God whom he often symbolized as Light. Between God and humans, Christ is the mediator: Christ transmits the holiness, light, beauty, and graciousness of God to sinful, darkened, helpless human beings. Because Christ shares in both the nature of God and the nature of human beings, he is able to bring the divine Spirit into our humanness and our humanness into the presence of God.

The goal of the Christian life is to live in God, to be in a deep, profound relationship with God. For Gregory, this relationship occurred through Christ, who, like the sun, shines in the darkness of human hearts. As the Son of God enlightens human consciousness, the night of sinfulness fades, and we are filled with streams of divine light. I have outlined Gregory's theological vision because it provides the framework for his discussion of the Word of God.

The primary way this inner transformation takes place is through our encounter with the Word, which comes to us in the bread and wine of communion and in the words of Scripture. In both instances the same Word encounters us. In meditation the texts of Scripture give us the means to think deeply about Christ. As we meditate upon this word, Christ speaks to us by the Spirit. As Gregory said, "The Son is the Word, but the Spirit is the tongue, through which the Son speaks."

As we continue to meditate upon Scripture, we will be led into a relationship of peace and stillness before God. Gregory does not understand meditation as a technique which, if properly practiced, will guarantee a relationship with God. Rather, meditation postures us toward God, and the text informs our thinking and praying, but there is no demand placed upon God by our disciplines. The human cannot manipulate the Holy.

So we must approach the posture of prayerful meditation on Scripture with a spirit of poverty and humility. We cannot pry open the gates of heaven by force, but, like indentured servants, we must be led into God's house. Because of the poverty of our situation, we grow in a profound relationship with God through humility, self-forgetfulness, and love. Gregory, like many of his monastic counterparts, spoke of this relationship as "union with God." For me, a child of the Reformation, it is difficult to conceive of union with God; as I see it, the human and the Holy don't get mingled together that way. But perhaps Gregory was speaking about a relationship, a kind of intimacy that occurs between parents and their children, or between lover and beloved. As the Son relates with the Father and the Father with the Son and with the Spirit, we enter into this relationship through the contemplation of the Word of God.

Is it true? Is it possible to have a vision of God, to be in union with God, to have the divine life within us? When Gregory speaks of vision, he makes it clear that he does not always mean seeing. It is one thing to look, but another to see. But, contends Gregory, a look indicates a desire to see, even if it does not behold its object. Whatever vision you or I may have marks the beginning of the final vision, either here or in the presence of God.

When Gregory speaks of a vision, he does not mean "vision" in the normal sense, because vision as he defines it does not involve images. Neither does vision involve rational analysis; rather, it suggests a union of see-er with the seen. Good works cannot earn vision, nor can ascetic practices create a vision, but we can prepare for it by recollecting who we are and what the aim of our life is, by meditating on Scripture, and by purifying our desires and motives. Certainly we do not demand this gift of God, but God chooses whomever he wills and reveals his nature according to his purposes.

Gregory provides this theological framework for our encounter with Scripture, and he makes clear that the aim is intimacy with God. How do we put Gregory's insights into our frame of reference? It seems to me that he defines our human predicament rather grimly — alienation from God, lives of darkness and misdirection. Christ has brought us back to God through his death and resurrection. In those pre-Reformation days, Gregory may not have seen the role of faith as clearly as we do.

But our concern with Gregory relates specifically to the use of Scripture. Scripture mediates the divine presence to us in the same way the sacraments of baptism and the Eucharist do. Indeed, Gregory holds a high view of Scripture and its role in the growth of the Spirit in us.

Gregory contends that as we read the texts of the Evangelists or the Apostle Paul, Christ meets us. As we meditate — think about, mull over, or ask questions of the text — Christ engages us in ever-increasing depth. These engagements with Christ through the texts make us conscious of his love, his gifts, and his gracious providence. In these sacred encounters,

Christ also brings to our consciousness our sin and disobedience, to which we confess and for which we seek healing.

Affirmation from Christ and cleansing by his Spirit through the Word lead to growth and conformity to Christ. Paul's metaphors of "Christ living in me" and "joined to Christ" seem to be what Gregory means by union. If we continue down this pathway, increasingly our minds and hearts will manifest Christ. Christ thinks his thoughts through us, loves the neighbor through us, and wills the Father's will in us. Although Calvin may not have quite the optimism of Gregory, he certainly emphasizes the testimony of the Spirit through the Word and our conformity to Christ.

Through our persistent meditation on the Word, our inner life with its shadows and darkness is revealed to us. Confession and cleansing open our souls to the light of God, which dispels the darkness. This light of the Spirit shining in the depths of our consciousness makes our relation with God deeper and richer. At some point along the journey, perhaps our hearts come to rest in God, and we "see" without images. What a marvelous place to reach on our journey — to have a relationship with God and a vision of him that fill us with gratitude and joy.

A Way of Meditation

From Gregory we learn that life before God gains enrichment and substance through meditation on Scripture. But his strong affirmations leave us with questions about meditation. What does it mean? How do we posture ourselves to do it? Why use a method?

One ancient way of meditating on Scripture has been called *Lectio Divina,* or spiritual reading. This method may have originated in the desert of Egypt, the devotional life in Antioch, or the intellectual center of Alexandria. No one is quite sure. But by the sixth century, it guided the daily prayer life of the monks under the care of Saint Benedict (c. 480-547). Besides performing the daily office of praying the Psalms and listening to the reading of Scripture, the monks of Benedict spent extended periods each day meditating on various texts. Their method was *Lectio Divina.* As these monks made their way through the Bible, meditating and reflecting on each word and phrase, it is little wonder that they memorized great portions of Scripture. Some say that Benedict required all his monks to memorize the whole New Testament and the Psalms.

Lectio Divina indicates a slow, studied, reflective way of reading a text from the Bible. The point is not how many verses of Scripture you read; you read not for information but for communion with Christ. The mind is more receptive than active; you seek to let the text find you rather than seeking a new insight or truth.

This method of meditation does not automatically produce union with God. Following the technique does not necessarily result in an encounter with Christ. This disclaimer parallels Gregory's conviction that our relationship with God is a gift, not something earned or manipulated by our techniques. While there is a defined order in *Lectio Divina,* it is not rigid.

This way of encountering God through Scripture has four movements: *lectio, meditatio, oratio,* and *contemplatio.* These four Latin words easily translate into "read," "meditate," "pray," and "contemplate." These four movements most likely emerged out of the devotional life of the faithful. The monks in the desert, for example, did not name these four movements as a formal system; rather, I suspect, they noticed what happened to them as they read Scripture.

First, they read a text and thought about it with a listening heart.

Second, as they thought about the text from different perspectives, parts of their lives were illumined by the light of the text, and this deeper awareness generated material for further thought. Meditation on the text brought them closer and closer to themselves and to the divine presence.

Third, when the text connected with a specific need in their lives, they prayed about it. As they prayed, deeper insights came and opened their lives even more.

Fourth, as they were drawn into the text, their attention shifted from themselves to God. In contemplation they were drawn into a deeper and deeper communion with God, which Gregory calls union with God. Contemplation led not only to communion but to vision — not a vision of images like hallucinations, but an inner vision of the Divine.

Over time, as they noticed these four movements, they began deliberately to engage the text in this fashion. When the faithful followers of Christ found a way of living before God that nurtured the soul, they shared it with other companions along the way.

This method of Scripture reading and meditation has been illustrated in various ways. Someone has described it as being like a cow eating grass. First the cow grazes in the field, cutting grass with her teeth. This is like reading the text. Second, the cow chews the grass and swallows it.

These two movements are similar to meditation and prayer. After the cow has filled her stomach, she stands around chewing her cud, an act of regurgitating the grass and chewing it again. This is an act similar to contemplation.

Another has compared *Lectio* to eating a grape. First, you take the grape in your hand; you look at it, turning it from side to side. Second, you place the grape on your lips or in your mouth; you might roll it around on your tongue for a moment. Third, you begin to chew the grape, breaking it into smaller and smaller parts as you chew. When you have chewed the grape thoroughly, you swallow it. Fourth, the grape that you have eaten makes its way into your stomach, to be converted into food for the body; it becomes a part of you. Thus the process of *Lectio* is like eating a grape: through it we aim to receive Christ through the medium of Scripture and metabolize his life into our own.

By the sixth century, *Lectio Divina* had become well-established in the devotional life of the church. Gregory the Great doubtless practiced this way of prayer during his years as a Benedictine monk. Perhaps his own experience was the reason he made meditation on Scripture so essential for communion with God.

I believe we would do well to embrace this clear, simple practice in our efforts to live in the presence of God today. For one thing, *Lectio* has a long and well-practiced history. But it also ties us to the text of Scripture in ways that Protestants appreciate. Perhaps the most compelling reason for our reading Scripture in this way comes from its connecting us with God.

In the life of devotion, Protestants too often never get out of their heads; they spend all their efforts on reading and understanding the text. Catholic mystics, by contrast, may leap from a word of the text into the contemplation of God. In the first instance, the experience of God remains rational claims; in the second, the relation with God lacks cognitive, theological grounding. The clearly ordered movement from reading the text to contemplating God provides a corrective to both of these deficiencies.

The Practice of *Lectio Divina*

I think the best way to make the practice of *Lectio Divina* accessible is to provide a model of the practice step by step. Look over my shoulder and watch how I engaged a portion of Scripture in this fourfold fashion.

I began with the selection of a short passage of Scripture. For this exercise I chose the metaphor of the vine and the branches:

> "I am the true vine, and my Father is the vinegrower. He removes every branch in me that bears no fruit. Every branch that bears fruit he prunes to make it bear more fruit. You have already been cleansed by the word that I have spoken to you. Abide in me as I abide in you. Just as the branch cannot bear fruit by itself unless it abides in the vine, neither can you unless you abide in me. I am the vine, you are the branches. Those who abide in me and I in them bear much fruit, because apart from me you can do nothing. Whoever does not abide in me is thrown away like a branch and withers; such branches are gathered, thrown into the fire, and burned. If you abide in me, and my words abide in you, ask for whatever you wish, and it will be done for you. My Father is glorified by this, that you bear much fruit and become my disciples." (John 15:1-8)

First, I read the passage slowly and reflectively. I noted the words and phrases that grasped my attention.

As I read this passage, several phrases captured my interest:

"I am the true vine."
"Abide in me as I abide in you."
"Apart from me you can do nothing."
"If you abide in me, and my words abide in you, ask for whatever you wish, and it will be done for you."

With the selection of these lines, I completed the first movement of encountering this passage. I listened to the words that spoke to me.

Second, I meditated on the text. Meditation is a deliberate act of thinking about the text, asking questions of it, turning it over in my mind to let it attract parts of my life. Meditation unearthed more material for prayer as I moved beyond the surface thoughts that arose when I read the text. These were my reflections:

> "Apart from me you can do nothing." What does it mean to depend upon you for strength and guidance? I have conversed with you about this great truth many times. Is there more for me to see?
>
> What things am I doing now, what ministries am I attempting? At

36

present I am developing a Certificate Program in Spiritual Formation for clergy and laypersons. I am also in conversation with other seminaries about offering this program to their constituency. We have begun the Certificate in Spiritual Formation for Master of Divinity students at Columbia Theological Seminary. I also dream of our offering a master's degree in spiritual direction. These ministries lie at the heart of my work life.

Without Christ I can do nothing in these programs. I may be able to dream of programs, create curricula, and promote this work in an effective way, but if it does not come from Christ, it is of no value. Without him I can do nothing!

What are my hopes and dreams for all these ministries in spirituality? Do I wish to enhance the reputation of Columbia Theological Seminary? Am I seeking to build a kingdom of my own? I know myself quite well, and if I labor for a fading glory, I am not aware of it. I don't claim perfection or absolute purity of motive because such is not possible. I care about the church, particularly my own Presbyterian Church (USA). I dream of renewed pastors and vibrant lay leaders who become salt, leaven, and light in the church. My hope rests on Christ, that he is involved with these modest efforts to renew his church. Without him I can do nothing.

What should I note in my life with him? All my life I have been interested in being a faithful disciple. As I review my life, I see patches of shameful failure that I regret. For the last two decades of my life I have felt a deep yearning for Christ, for his will in my life. I have practiced a variety of disciplines, devoted myself to his work, and prayed much about being a trustworthy disciple. In this text I see all my efforts count for nothing apart from Christ. Whatever invitations of his I have responded to, whatever motions of the Spirit have moved me, and whatever grace has been shown to me is all that matters. Without him I can do nothing!

Does this inability mean that I should sink into passivity? No, I don't think so. The way of Christ is so strange. You're never quite sure whether you are doing a ministry or Christ is doing it through you. To say it another way, he works through us when he chooses, and most often we don't know whether it is him or us!

Asking the questions about "apart from me you can do nothing" was my way of meditating on the text. Notice how meditation took me

37

to a deeper level of thinking, feeling, and prayer. At the moment I felt that my soul had been penetrated and opened up, like an envelope being sliced open by a letter opener. I felt disrobed and exposed. (Each of the other phrases I selected could also have become the subject of meditation. This single illustration, however, makes clear the second movement in *Lectio Divina* and prepares the way for the next movement, *oratio*.)

Third, I prayed about the way in which the text connected with my life today. These were my thoughts when I let the text into my heart:

"I am the true vine." Jesus is the true source of my life. All that has meaning and value for me springs from him. But I see myself often turning to other so-called sources of life. Some days I turn to my own strength as the source, and my life goes dry. I find my mind filled with thoughts of my own security in what I possess. Lord, you are the source of my life. Keep pruning these wild sprouts and renewing my sense of your presence.

"Abide in me as I abide in you." As I read this text again, you seemed to be answering my prayer from the "true vine" text. My secret is to abide in you, to rest my soul in your hands. You do not say anything about pruning more from my life but about focusing my awareness on you, remaining centered in you. I note that you say, ". . . as I abide in you." Because I am grafted into you, the "true vine," you are already abiding in me, and now you invite me to notice that you are inside me. You desire me to be in you the same way. Indeed, this is a mystery to me.

"Apart from me you can do nothing." How prone I am to think that I can do your work with my own strength. Once again you are reminding me that "the work of God can only be done by God." Yet, as I listen to you, your words are not judging, nor are they condemning. I hear you speaking a gentle reminder to me that I gladly hear. I hear you suggesting "with me, all things are possible."

"If you abide in me, and my words abide in you, ask for whatever you wish, and it will be done for you." What a promise! What words of assurance! You bring me back to the central focus for my life — abiding in you — and then you offer me the promise that I can ask for anything, and it will be granted. Somehow you know that when I abide in you (as you are already abiding in me), I cannot ask for wild and crazy things. Abiding in you and your word abiding in me inform what I am to ask. My prayer becomes your prayer in me, and your prayers to the Father are always answered.

As I recall what you have said to me in these texts, I see clearly that you are the source of my life. From you comes who I am, what I am to do — my very being comes from you. And when I rest in you as you constantly rest in me, I remain connected to the source of my life. Apart from your presence in me and your power that operates through me, I can do nothing of value for your Kingdom. But when I abide in you and your words take root in my life, I have the privilege of asking for anything (yes, anything), and it will be given to me. Thanks to you, O Christ, for this, your word to me.

Notice how prayer returns to meditation, and meditation expresses itself in prayer. The reflection on the affirmation "I am the true vine" began with my thinking objectively about Christ, but soon my consciousness changed from "thinking about" Christ to "being in conversation with" Christ.

Fourth, I contemplated the text. Contemplation begins with the text but uses it as a means to enter into the presence of Christ (God). At this moment I am aware that my structured way of being in the world has been penetrated by the Word of Christ. He has brought to my mind the things for which I need his help, both in my vocational life and in my personal life. I can do nothing apart from him. Realizing this, I deeply desire to enter into his presence and be before him.

My way into the presence will lead me beyond thoughts about my "nothingness," my feelings of helplessness, and all my ideas about being a faithful disciple of Christ. Contemplation constitutes a state of being beyond thoughts, feelings, desires, and intentions. The way into contemplation demands "letting go" of everything but our awareness of and love for him.

In my act of contemplation, I closed my eyes and began to think about two texts alternately: "Apart from you can do nothing" and "With me all things are possible." I repeated these in mantra-like fashion two or three times. Then the words began to fall away, and I found myself saying, "Nothing. Possible. Nothing. Possible." Finally, all words left, and I was in the Other Dimension.

Distractions began to multiply: my wife walking across the floor upstairs, a plane flying overhead. I wondered how to get my mind focused again.

After struggling with these distractions, I turned toward an image of Christ in white that I envisioned. There seems to be a place in the depth of my soul where I often meet him. I went to this center, and he was there, but nothing unusual happened.

Frustrated by my failure to get quiet inside, to focus my attention upon Christ, I began to let go of my own efforts. As my efforts subsided, I had a sense that he was aware of me, whether or not I had a profound consciousness of him.

For a few moments I was aware of his being aware of me. In those moments I had no thoughts, no striving, no hungers or fears, only peace.

Again I was interrupted — this time by the phone's ringing and my wife's coming downstairs.

At that moment I was enjoying the contemplation of the divine presence, a sense of being connected to Christ, a peace about myself and my life.

As you study this model of *Lectio Divina,* remember that I've written about one experience on a particular day. Don't think of this description as a formula or an example meant to be normative. You shouldn't try to imitate my experience. I offer you this model simply to provide you with an approach to each of the four movements in *Lectio Divina.*

Lectio Divina Shared in Community

I doubt if the old monks of the desert shared *lectio* in community, but in more recent times, small groups of seekers have found it helpful. Several years ago my associate led our spiritual formation class in an experience of *Lectio Divina.* After having studied *Lectio Divina* as an individual devotional approach to Scripture, she introduced us to a group approach. I'm not sure whether she conceived this idea or borrowed it from someone else; perhaps she had participated in a group that used it. So I describe it with an apology, not knowing its origin.

Lectio
Reading God's Word

1. One person reads aloud (twice) the chosen passage of Scripture, as others in the group attend to some portion that is especially meaningful to them.
2. Silence is observed for one to two minutes. Each person silently repeats a word or phrase that attracted his or her attention.
3. Sharing aloud: Each person repeats that word or phrase without elaboration.

Meditatio
Reflecting on God's Word

1. A second person reads the same Scripture passage.
2. Silence is observed for two to three minutes. Each participant reflects on the question "Where does the content of this reading touch my life today?"
3. Sharing aloud: Each person briefly shares what the reading means to him or her: "I hear . . . ," "I see . . . ," "I was struck by . . ."

Oratio
Responding to God

1. A third person reads the same Scripture passage.
2. Silence is observed for two to three minutes. All reflect on how God is calling them to respond.
3. Sharing aloud: Each person says a brief, spontaneous prayer, expressing his or her response to God's call.

Contemplatio
Resting in God

1. A fourth person reads the same Scripture passage.
2. Participants rest in the Word, in silence for two to three minutes.
3. All say aloud, "Our Father . . ."

Operatio
Responding in Action

1. A fifth person reads the same Scripture passage.
2. Silence is observed for one to two minutes. Each person reflects on the question "What does the Lord want me to do? Which word or phrase will I take with me?"
3. Sharing aloud: Each person briefly shares the word or phrase that calls him or her to action.

Closure

Do you see how this way of encountering Christ through Scripture can begin to shape you spiritually? Do you see how this practice will sharpen your awareness of his presence in you? And do you now understand how this way of reading Scripture will furnish you with criteria for discernment? All these signs of growth come to us as we seek Christ in the Word of Scripture.

Consider ways that you may fruitfully use this approach to reading Scripture in your personal discipline, but also consider groups to whom you may introduce it.

Questions for Reflection and Discussion

1. How does the Bible communicate the presence of God?
2. What are the reasons for reading and meditating on Scripture?
3. What is the sequence of appropriating Scripture in *Lectio Divina?* How does this compare or contrast with your usual way of reading Scripture?

A Journaling Exercise

1. Choose a brief passage of Scripture. Using the example in the chapter, record your experience of reading, meditating on, praying about, and contemplating the chosen text.
2. When you finish, write a reflection on your experience of *Lectio Divina.*

CHAPTER FOUR

Resisting the Biggest Lie

The effort to live before God exposes us to a perennial lie, a questioning of the truth that reaches far back into human memory. The greatest lie, as I will call it, was born simultaneously with human consciousness. Exposure to this perversion of reality poses a threat to all of us from the dawn of consciousness right up to its flickering out with our last breath. Sometimes this lie seems so close to us that we cannot escape it; it is as if it has been woven into our longing for the Ultimate Truth.

This lie echoes in our ears before we come to a living faith; it intrudes into our awareness as we contemplate the direction of our lives; it haunts us when we consider our destiny to live as open, obedient servants of the most high God.

What is the greatest lie? In some sense, every temptation comes down to a question of trust. Before you too quickly dismiss this assertion, consider the possibility of our mistrusting hearts. What was the temptation of our forebears? Was it not to turn away from God, to doubt the integrity and faithfulness of God? As God's people, we must posture ourselves with a marked trust in God's integrity. Adam and Eve knew this, but they allowed the serpent to mislead them. Let's review that account from our earliest tradition:

The First Temptation

Now the serpent was more crafty than any other wild animal that the LORD God had made. He said to the woman, "Did God say, 'You

43

shall not eat from any tree in the garden'?" The woman said to the serpent, "We may eat of the fruit of the trees in the garden; but God said, 'You shall not eat of the fruit of the tree that is in the middle of the garden, nor shall you touch it, or you shall die.'"

But the serpent said to the woman, "You will not die; for God knows that when you eat of it your eyes will be opened, and you will be like God, knowing good and evil." So when the woman saw that the tree was good for food, and that it was a delight to the eyes, and that the tree was to be desired to make one wise, she took of its fruit and ate; and she also gave some to her husband, who was with her, and he ate. Then the eyes of both were opened, and they knew that they were naked; and they sewed fig leaves together and made loincloths for themselves.

They heard the sound of the LORD God walking in the garden at the time of the evening breeze, and the man and his wife hid themselves from the presence of the LORD God among the trees of the garden. But the LORD God called to the man, and said to him, "Where are you?"

He said, "I heard the sound of you in the garden, and I was afraid, because I was naked; and I hid myself." (Gen. 3:1-10)

This bedrock narrative in the opening pages of the Hebrew Scriptures points to the original temptation — to doubt the integrity and veracity of the Creator God. It matters little whether you read this story as a historical account of "the Fall," or a piece of ancient literature, or a myth — the implied meaning is the same. At the dawn of human consciousness, an Alien Voice — whether that of a crafty animal, Satan, or the Devil, it matters not — questioned the integrity of God.

The Alien's case went something like this. "Did God say that you shall not eat from any tree in the garden?" Quickly the woman responded, "Oh no, we may eat of the fruit of all the trees except the one in the midst of the garden. If we touch or eat from that tree, we shall die."

Again, the Alien attacked the veracity of God. "You will not die. God knows that if you eat from this tree, you will become like God." Not only did the enemy deny God's word to the original pair, but he hinted that God could not be trusted, that God was withholding participation in deity from the man and the woman. Eating the fruit of the tree in the midst of the garden would make them godlike. God could not be trusted to be God and grant them communion with God's self.

Our forebears believed the lie, ate the fruit, and suffered the consequences of alienation from themselves, from each other, and from God. This brokenness always occurs when we turn from the true God to ourselves as god. Like the primal pair, we too are afraid when God speaks our name.

At the core of this debacle stands the simple issue of trust. You cannot trust the goodness of God; you cannot trust the purposes of God; you cannot trust God to meet your needs even if you live faithfully. From that day until this, human beings have been vulnerable to the garden temptation, have been inclined to distrust the goodness, integrity, and faithfulness of God to fulfill completely the divine purpose.

The Devil placed a dark question mark in the minds of our human parents when he said, "God knows that when you eat of it your eyes will be opened, and you will be like God, knowing good and evil."

Do You Believe in the Devil?

But wait! Maybe I'm moving too fast for you. Do you believe in the Devil? I have been confronted with that issue myself.

I had been invited to assist a congregation with spiritual growth and congregational renewal. Sessions generally began with a lecture followed by questions and answers or small-group sharing and prayer. On the first evening, I had finished speaking to the group and was standing at the door, bidding good night to those who had attended, when a woman confronted me, asking, "Do you believe in a personal Devil?"

"I think that I would say, 'I believe in a force of evil in the world.'"

"Well," she said, "if you don't believe in a personal Devil, can you really believe in a personal God?"

Her question rocked me a bit. "I think you can believe in God without believing in a personal Devil," I answered, "but I do believe there is a power, a force that opposes God and all that God wills to do in the world."

"Well, I'm glad to hear you say that," she responded, "because if you don't believe in a personal Devil, I can't sit this whole weekend and listen to you speak!"

When I went home that evening, I asked myself questions that arose out of this unexpected encounter. Did I really believe in a personal Devil? What is he like? (I don't suppose you mind if I make him masculine, do you?) Is there an alien power at work in the world and in

45

human hearts? What does the Bible say? What experience have I had of this evil one?

A friend of mine who had serious doubts about the Devil chaired the Billy Graham Crusade in Atlanta in the early seventies. On the night before the crusade opened, he entertained Mr. Graham and the crusade staff. During dinner, my friend casually remarked that he didn't believe in a personal Devil.

In a pleasant manner and with a charming smile, Mr. Graham replied, "Before this crusade is over, you will."

The next day, my friend told me, strange things began to happen. First, the planners had arranged for the rapid transit system to pick up folks at designated locations across the city. On the night the crusade began, the bus drivers went on a wildcat strike. They struck for three days.

Next, one of our controversial black leaders in Atlanta seized the opportunity to make the headlines of the local newspapers. He declared the crusade was the white man's religion and that blacks were being co-opted. He called on African-Americans to surround the stadium and dare any black person to cross the picket line.

And then came yet another blow. The planners had installed a good public-address system as well as a backup. On the very first night of the crusade, both the primary system and the backup system had bugs in them, and the audience could barely interpret the garbled speech they heard. My friend concluded his story by saying, "And that was the week that I began to believe in the Devil."

I'm not claiming that these mishaps prove the existence of the Devil, but I am suggesting that the three major problems that befell the crusade cause me to wonder.

A few summers ago I read *Dark Debts,* a novel by Karen Hall, a part-time resident of Atlanta. One small section of the story got at the issue of belief in the Devil. To capture Hall's point, I'm summarizing several pages here.[1]

In this scene, two priests were attempting an exorcism — casting out the Devil. It was not as dramatic as the scene in *The Exorcist* (the film), but in the dialogue between Bob, the older priest who conducted the exorcism, and Michael, the younger, skeptical priest, Hall raised the issues that many moderns deal with concerning the Devil.

While they were preparing to engage in the exorcism, the subject

---

1. Karen Hall, *Dark Debts* (New York: Random House, 1996), pp. 194-203.

spoke with a demonic voice and unmasked the most private, hidden sins in Michael's life. He was staggered by the revelations. He left the room, convinced that he had been confronted with the presence and power of evil. The dialogue between them went something like this:

"Make it make sense!" Michael said to Bob.

"You believe in the concept of spirit because you believe in God." Bob began.

"Yes."

"If you believe in a benevolent spirit," Bob continued, "why do you have trouble believing in an evil spirit?"

"Well," Michael responded, "I find myself throwing around terms like 'Lucifer,' 'Satan,' 'Christ casting out demons,' but I think of them metaphorically. But tell me, Bob — do you believe in the Devil?"

"I don't believe in a little red guy with horns and a pitchfork," Bob answered. "I think it's all pretty complex, perhaps with layers of evil. I can think of at least two kinds of evil — the evil in human beings and the larger evil beyond them. I think they parallel the hierarchy of heaven — God, saints, and angels, and Satan, demons, and lesser demons.

"What Satan looks like I don't know, any more than I know what God looks like. What I do know is that when the big E (evil) finds a doorway into the human realm and communicates on a level we understand, it's not some vague, nebulous force. It's right there, in the room, in your face. It's individual, personal."

The way this author describes the power of evil seems to match a great deal of my understanding and experience. I don't believe in "a little red guy with horns and a pitchfork," but I do believe there is a power of evil that communicates in a manner we understand and by which we are challenged and sometimes oppressed.

What about you? Have there been times in your life when the Force, this Voice from Darkness, spoke to you, challenging the things you most deeply believe? Can you not recall times that this negative, "in your face," "personal" power of evil seemed to be there, telling you what to do, what to believe, what to doubt? And for you to have obeyed that voice would have been a tragic mistake!

The Devil as a Liar

In a confrontation with the Jews, Jesus made clear the nature of the one who opposes us and the will of God. Jesus described him as a liar, the father of lies, and one whose nature is corrupt and deceitful. The voice that opposes us lies to us. John records Jesus' encounter with the Jews in these words:

> Jesus said to them, "If God were your Father, you would love me, for I came from God and now I am here. I did not come on my own, but he sent me. Why do you not understand what I say? It is because you cannot accept my word. You are from your father the devil, and you choose to do your father's desires. He was a murderer from the beginning and does not stand in the truth, because there is no truth in him. When he lies, he speaks according to his own nature, for he is a liar and the father of lies. But because I tell the truth, you do not believe me. Which of you convicts me of sin? If I tell the truth, why do you not believe me? Whoever is from God hears the words of God. The reason you do not hear them is that you are not from God." (John 8:42-47)

In this text Jesus unmasks the nature of the Alien Voice that speaks to us. He specifically addresses the Jewish leaders who are intent upon killing him. They claimed Abraham as their father, but Jesus underscored their illegitimacy by saying they were from their father, the Devil. Jesus identified the enemy of wholeness and fulfillment as "a liar and the father of lies." Deceptiveness is the chief characteristic Jesus attributed to the Devil.

Jesus himself knew from experience this Master Deceiver. He experienced him in the desert as the three primal temptations were hurled at him.

If you are the Son of God —

"Turn these stones into bread."

"Cast yourself down from the pinnacle of the temple. God will give his angels power to rescue you." Liar!

"All this world I will give you if you will fall down and worship me." Liar again!

If he is a liar and the father of all lies, he is out to deceive the whole world. What do you think those lies are?

He tells people there is no God. That's a lie, but it isn't the biggest lie.

48

Some have fallen for it, but most people only have to open their eyes and watch the sun set, the moon rise, or a flower grow to know this isn't true.

He tells people that God may exist but that he isn't involved in their lives. The deceiver would have us believe that God created the world, wound it up like a top, set it in motion, and retired to the other side of the galaxies. This is yet another lie, but not the biggest lie.

He tells people who are suffering that God could do something to alleviate their pain but won't. This is a lie, but not the biggest.

He tells other people, those who won't be swayed by the insensitivity of God, that God wishes to help them but can't. A big, big lie! But still not the biggest!

The Devil's biggest lie is something else. This one lie is the biggest because it affects the most people; it is the biggest because it is the most widespread; it is the biggest because of its great destructive power.

The biggest lie of the Devil is, *"You can't trust God to be God!"*

God cannot be trusted to care for us. God cannot be trusted to provide for our needs. God cannot be trusted when bad things happen to us. These and a thousand other lies attack the veracity of God. To shield our souls from this barrage of doubts, we take refuge in God's mercy.

Struggling with the Devil's Lies

I don't know of anyone who seriously seeks to live before God who is not confronted with the Alien Voice, the Voice that speaks confusion and doubt into the soul. The first Voice in the Bible is the Voice of the Creator, but the second is that of Chaos, which resists the creative word of God and seeks to undermine the confidence of those seeking to live faithfully in the Presence of the Holy One. I have met these persons in many places.

I had finished a talk at a church in California when this wonderful young woman came up to me. "Why am I afraid to listen to God?" she asked me.

"I don't know," I answered. "Why do you think you are?"

"I think," she said, "that I'm afraid of what God might say to me."

"What do you think that would be?"

"I think that it would be the thing that I most dread, the thing that I most fear, or the thing that I would never want to do."

"And that keeps you from listening to God?" I asked.

She had been frightened by the biggest lie of the Devil: You can't trust God to be God. The Devil says, "If you give your life over to God, if you give God permission to do with you as God wills, God will immediately command you to do the worst thing imaginable." Is this really the character of God?

I have had my own struggles with this Alien Voice. When I was in college, I was terrified that God would call me to Africa, because that was the last place I wanted to go. Being called to be a missionary in another country was my greatest fear. So when the college had mission conferences, I refused to go. I reasoned that if I wasn't at the conference, God couldn't call me. My fear arose because I didn't trust God to be God. Surely God knew my gifts and where they could best be used, and a good, loving God would seek not to destroy my life but to use and fulfill it.

Some people in their experience of pain, misfortune, and despair begin to believe the lie that God cannot be trusted. When they face evil with a capital "E," they don't have the power to deny or resist the lie.

Not long ago I had a student named Janie who, in the face of enormous evil, stood fast and resisted every lie that was hurled at her. If ever there was a person who had a reason to believe the Devil's biggest lie, she did. She was reared in an abusive home in which her father and mother fought constantly; her father disciplined her and her siblings, even mentally tortured them. Her mother, seeking help, counseled with her conservative minister, who persuaded her to stay married to her cruel husband.

At fifteen, Janie came home to a family fight and watched as her father attacked her mother with a sharp kitchen knife. Terrified, she ran and jumped on her father's back, trying to stop the killing. When she looked into his eyes, she couldn't see a person inside, only darkness. She was terrified and overwhelmed as she looked at him, and yet she did not utter a sound. Her father killed her mother right before her eyes. He was tried and convicted but spent only a few years behind bars. Wouldn't these experiences test your trust in a good God?

Janie left home at an early age and went to New York to make it big as a singer — but she didn't. After failing, she loaded her car with her mikes and music boards (boards especially designed for her voice that were worth about $25,000) and returned to her apartment to pick up one last thing before heading home. When she got back to her parking space, she realized someone had stolen her car and everything she had, including the expensive music boards. (What kind of power in the universe could permit this?)

This tragedy came on the heels of another significant loss. A few months before, she had made a trip to California with her fiancé. He died from a heart attack shortly after they returned. It seemed that one catastrophe after another, like waves of a raging sea, hit her before she could get back up.

After two years she returned to New York City to make a religious record, but the studio hired strippers to be the backup singers. It was too much of a contradiction for her, and she bailed out of the project.

While still in New York City, she got a good job in consulting with a computer company, and she advanced quickly and was paid a large salary. Management asked her to move to Chicago for more money than she had ever heard of. Just before leaving New York City, she was walking to McDonald's to get a drink, and then on to Central Park to roller-blade. On the way to the park, she put on her skates. She fell, seriously fracturing her leg; it swelled to twice the size of mine.

Her minister came to visit her after she returned home from the hospital. He asked with sharp interest, "What have you always wanted to do?"

She said, "Work in the church and serve God." (Can you imagine it?)

"Do it," he urged. So she came to Atlanta and Columbia Seminary to begin her preparation.

Can't you imagine the demonically inspired conversation that went on in her head? "If God wants what is good for you, why did he permit your mother to stay with your father? Why did he permit your father to kill your mother before your eyes? Why did he allow your fiancé to die? Why did God let those hoodlums steal your property? And about that job — why did God let you break your leg? Is God there? Does God love you? Could anything worse happen to you? Don't you feel the weight of betrayal in these questions?"

In the power of Christ, this child of God said, "No. I don't believe you. I trust my life to God." What an amazing power is released in our lives when we let go and let God.

Facing the Question

When you decide seriously to seek God's Kingdom, I can promise you, without much fear of contradiction, an encounter with the Enemy of all souls. I doubt that you will get through life without asking the question, "Can God be trusted?" Perhaps you will not deal with multiple losses like my student faced, but you will face losses, and the question will naturally arise.

51

Each of us lives in an ordered world of our own making; we have a picture of how things are and how we expect them to be. Then some unexpected event occurs like the loss of a job, the death of someone close, or a life-threatening illness. Life cannot go on as you planned; your expectations have been dashed. When life shatters your picture of reality, all the barriers that keep out the chaos break down. Consequently, you stagger under the deluge, and questions mixed with fear fill your mind. Why? Why me? Where is God? Can I trust God now?

When I have faced these moments of chaos, I have first tried to run away, to pretend that the chaotic experience isn't happening to me. But when I have run, the chaos has always overtaken me. After a significant number of failures, it has become obvious to me that running will not relieve my confusion and fears.

As difficult as it may be, I find it better to face my darkness or emptiness or confusion and admit my feelings to myself and to God. I try to own my negative feelings and deal with the inevitable question: "Can I trust God when everything in me denies there is a God?"

To suppress this question or to pretend it doesn't haunt you will only lead to self-deception. Denial in turn leads to phoniness. Even if you conceal your fears behind a pious mask, you still know the questions lie dormant inside.

A further mistake I have made has been to argue with the Tempter. My line of reasoning has often been that I don't really have to struggle with this question. Or that I have trusted God in the past and others have trusted God, so I can trust God now. These arguments about being able to trust God are true, but they don't bring relief to a troubled heart.

I have found that the simplest and most honest way of confronting the issue of trust lies in waiting and resting. Usually, after I have acknowledged my true condition before God, I begin to hear voices in my head that say, "If God . . ." or "Why did God . . . ?" These questions, if you permit them, will initiate an argument with the Evil One that you cannot win.

When the debate begins, I stop it by saying, "I will not argue this issue with you. I belong to God, and God will not forsake me." End of debate.

I then look to God. I let the loss, the confusion, and the questions turn me to God. When I'm able to take this posture, I change the contention of the Evil One into the contemplation of God. I wait before God with openness and an expectation that God will show me the way through the crisis. Thus far, God has never failed.

Questions for Reflection and Discussion

1. How do you understand the meaning of the Devil or Satan?

2. What is the meaning of Jesus' struggle with the Devil in the desert?

3. Can you think of times you felt tempted to distrust the goodness of God? Do my suggestions of how to deal with the experience help you?

4. Is it true that "mistrusting the goodness of God" lies at the heart of every temptation?

A Journaling Exercise

1. Make a list of the times you have been tested.

2. Choose one of these testing periods to work with in your journal. Regarding that time in your life, write, "It was a time when . . ."

3. Complete this sentence about that experience: "When I was tempted . . ."

4. Write a short paragraph describing what you learned from this experience.

CHAPTER FIVE

Listening for God

Living before God means being in communion with God, sharing the deepest feelings and hungers of our lives with One who knows us, knows all about us. For too long, many of us have had conversation from one side only — ours — and we have not expected an answer from Beyond. But from Beyond a Voice speaks, and we learn to listen to the many sounds from the One before whom we live to assume a posture of openness and alertness to catch the sounds of the Spirit.

How often we forget that speech defines the character of this One who inhabits the Beyond. God is the God who speaks. If we are to believe the biblical record, this self-communicating God takes the initiative to engage us and speak the words we need to hear. This Other One breaks the sound barriers, interrupts the silence, and communicates to us in our situation through ever-changing media. Metaphorically, "voice" refers not only to throat and vocal cords but also to signs, symbols, and movements. Listeners for God must always have an ear cocked, we might say, to learn the language of the One who continually speaks.

The ways of "godspeech" cannot be numbered, so many are there, but even the casual reader of Scripture can recognize amazing variety. In our attempts to learn the posture of listening, we will discover God's solitary speech. Very soon we will discover that the solitary God engages us in dialogical speech, that God is the One who not only speaks but also listens. And then we will recognize that this God speaks not only through our intuitive, imaginative grasping of indirect speech, but through the clearly anointed voice of Another. Our learning the ways of godspeech will lead us to explore the symbolic, communicative power of litany and liturgy that expresses the Word of the self-revealing God.

Solitary Speech

On the opening page of the Bible, we encounter God's solitary speech. Without provocation from anything or anyone, this lone Voice spoke:

> Then God said, "Let there be light"; and there was light. And God saw that the light was good; and God separated the light from the darkness. God called the light Day, and the darkness he called Night. And there was evening and there was morning, the first day. (Gen. 1:3-5)

This spontaneous speech marks the beginning of creation and introduces us to the God who speaks.

No one has ever penetrated the darkness before creation to find the reason for this initial word, "Let there be . . . ," and no one ever will. The purpose of creation has caused much speculation, and while there may be hints in history, the Bible, and even creation itself, God's purposes are still concealed in the divine mystery.

In the New Testament story of Jesus' life and ministry, we again encounter this solitary Voice. The Voice does not speak in response to anyone addressing or calling upon God. Early on, Jesus came to John for baptism, and a Voice spoke. The word spoken at the Baptism had its own reasons and provided its own initiative. Luke describes the Voice in these words:

> Now when all the people were baptized, and when Jesus also had been baptized and was praying, the heaven was opened, and the Holy Spirit descended upon him in bodily form like a dove. And a voice came from heaven, "You are my Son, the Beloved; with you I am well pleased." (Luke 3:21-22)

The spontaneous word — "You are my Son, the Beloved; with you I am well pleased" — gave Jesus clarity about his identity and marked the beginning of his ministry. I suppose you could argue that the obedience of Jesus pleased the Father and caused God to express divine pleasure, or you could say that Jesus' prayer evoked the Father's pleasure. But it seems to me that the Voice speaks spontaneously.

How is it that we so easily shrug off this solitary speech that comes spontaneously and so powerfully? Perhaps the Voice fails to get our attention because we expect a noisy display. Yet when God spoke at creation, there was no sound at all. And when God spoke at the Baptism, no one heard the Voice but Jesus.

Nevertheless, it was important for Jesus to hear the Voice because it confirmed his identity as Son of God and empowered him to face the temptations in the desert. Strange how each of the temptations focused on the issue of his identity. Each of the temptations began with "If you are the Son of God . . . ," which suggests three direct efforts to discredit God's declaration to Jesus.

Do we not also have these gentle, frequent, and spontaneous intrusions into our consciousness? Is this not one of the ways God speaks to us if we are listening?

I have kept no record of the various times that this spontaneous, solitary Voice has spoken to me, but it has done so frequently. Most of the time it requires careful discernment, especially when major issues are at stake. At other times the Voice speaks and seems quickly to add its own verification.

I recall one instance of this solitary disclosure while I was on retreat at the Monastery of the Holy Spirit outside Conyers, Georgia. I suppose I had been there for the better part of a day when I seated myself at a small desk to begin writing. As soon as I sat down, the Voice said, "Contact Richard Franks." The Voice spoke on Friday. I was impressed enough with the "word" to write the directive in my journal.

I knew Richard (not his real name), but we were not intimate friends. I had no idea why this directive had come to me, but I intended to follow through on it. As had happened before, my good intentions faded into neglect, and when Monday came I still had not made contact with Richard Franks. During a class on Tuesday, a group of students reported on a visit to Richard's church over the weekend. They didn't talk about anything going on in the church, but they mentioned the name of the pastor. No sooner had they uttered his name than my memory nudged me: "Contact Richard Franks."

That very day I called Richard. I felt a bit awkward when I began the conversation. "Richard, I feel somewhat nervous calling you out of the blue like this, but I had a strange thing happen to me at the Monastery last week." I told him about the Voice and my intention to obey its guidance.

57

He seemed to understand and gave no indication of being perturbed by a call more or less directed by God. Actually he seemed more relaxed in accepting the call than I did in making it. After a few minutes of exchanging greetings and apologies for being out of touch, Richard related his side of the story.

He began by asking, "Do you know what's going on in our congregation?"

"No, I don't know anything, except that I was told to call you."

With that explanation he began telling me about his situation.

"For several months," he said, "I have been confronted with a small group of people in the congregation who have been trying to get rid of me. The conflict began over a year ago, but a few months back one of my opponents entered my office, took my personal journal from my desk, and made copies of my recordings of personal struggles and poignant temptations. My adversaries distributed the entries in my journal to members of the congregation and turned my struggles and temptations into hideous sins. I have never faced greater humiliation in my life. Not only am I the victim of character assassination, but my associate minister has joined forces with those who are seeking my dismissal.

"This past Sunday night the struggle came to a head, and a committee from the denomination met with the personnel committee of our church. They requested that the associate minister resign immediately, and they asked me to begin looking for other employment this year.

"You see, Ben, I think there was good reason for someone to tell you to call Richard Franks. As a matter of fact, I take that word and your call as assurance that God has not forgotten about me in my struggle. Thanks."

An incident like this could be a sheer accident; the Enlightenment has taught me to think that way. But the manner in which this urge came to call Richard, the situation in which he found himself, and the timing indicate to me that something more profound was taking place. I can't prove that God directed me to call Richard, but I don't feel any need to do so. I am convinced that the One who spoke that solitary Word of Creation and that solitary Word at the Baptism still speaks those solitary, spontaneous, revelatory words to ordinary persons like us. Our task in living before God is learning to listen and discern.

Dialogical Speech

Paying attention to the spontaneous speech of God means that we must attend those gentle hints and directives that come to us from time to time. But this is not the only manner of listening to God. God speaks through the deep, inward impressions of the soul but also in response to our direct questions and concerns.

We first encounter this dialogical speech in the early chapters of Genesis. The conversation between God and Adam and Eve after they had eaten the fruit from the tree in the midst of the garden provides us the first example:

> They heard the sound of the LORD God walking in the garden at the time of the evening breeze, and the man and his wife hid themselves from the presence of the LORD God among the trees of the garden.
>
> But the LORD God called to the man, and said to him, "Where are you?" He said, "I heard the sound of you in the garden, and I was afraid, because I was naked; and I hid myself."
>
> He [God] said, "Who told you that you were naked? Have you eaten from the tree of which I commanded you not to eat?"
>
> The man said, "The woman whom you gave to be with me, she gave me fruit from the tree, and I ate."
>
> Then the LORD God said to the woman, "What is this that you have done?" The woman said, "The serpent tricked me, and I ate." (Gen. 3:8-13)

We have a narrative at the dawn of human consciousness that depicts a conversation between God and human beings. The whole Bible has been written on the premise that vital religion consists of an ongoing dialogue between God and humankind. In the Older Testament the dialogue took place between God and the nation Israel. In the Newer Testament the dialogue occurred between Christ and his followers, and subsequently between Christ and his church. When the earthly Jesus no longer walks in the flesh with his followers, his communication takes place through the Spirit.

I like to think of the Spirit as the universal presence of Christ. The resurrection of Christ liberated him from the bonds of time, and the ascension liberated him from the limitations of space. The pouring forth of the Spirit through the cosmos suggests that the risen Lord fillls all time and every place. This presence makes possible our continuous dialogue with him.

The experience of Saint Paul illustrates dialogical speech after Jesus' departure from the earth. Saint Paul spoke to the Lord about his thorn in the flesh. We are not quite certain what Paul's thorn was — whether it was his eyes, his height, or some physical malady. But whatever it was, Paul judged it a detriment to his service to Christ.

Paul reports, "Three times I appealed to the Lord about this, that it would leave me, but he said to me, 'My grace is sufficient for you, for power is made perfect in weakness.'"

"So," Paul responds, "I will boast all the more gladly of my weaknesses, so that the power of Christ may dwell in me" (2 Cor. 12:8-9).

This dialogue is brief, and I suspect we possess a highly condensed version of Paul's actual conversation. We do not know how this dialogue between Paul and Christ took place, but I suspect it was in the mind of Paul. He used his own vocabulary and thought processes to converse with Christ. Whoever we are and wherever we are — whether Adam and Eve in the garden, or the Israelites in the desert, or Saint Paul in Asia, or you and me today — living before God means entering into conversation with the One in whose presence we live.

This dialogical communication does still occur today. When persons are willing to set aside time, quiet themselves, and offer themselves to God in conversation, God's speech can be heard. Perhaps it will amaze you that God sometimes chooses to speak through our own lips.

The notion of God speaking to me through my own lips first came to me more than forty years ago. When I was a freshman in college, someone recommended to me Frank C. Laubach's little booklet entitled *Letters by a Modern Mystic.* At the time he wrote these letters, Dr. Laubach was serving as a missionary in the Philippines.

In the letters he describes how each evening he went up on Signal Hill, overlooking the city, and spoke with God. One evening after he had spoken to God, he felt an urge to open his mouth and lend his lips to the Lord. To his amazement, words began coming back through his own voice, words that seemed to come from God. These words were both assuring and prophetic. He states, "The newest experiment, and at present the most thrilling, is letting God talk through my own tongue and through my own fingers on the typewriter."

In the first few paragraphs below I have included the content of one revelation that Laubach received as he sat at his typewriter, transcribing the words that came to him. These may not be God's words flowing through his mind and hands, but before you decide one way or the other, read them over a few times.

Frank Laubach's Message

I speak to you, not through your tongue only, but also through everything which you see in nature: through the beauty of this sunset, through the little Moro boy who stands beside you without understanding what you are saying, and who wonders what you are looking at in the clouds.

If I do not speak to you in words at times, it is because the reality all about you is greater than the imperfect symbols of things which you have in words. It is not necessary for your tongue to speak, nor even for any definite thoughts to light your mind, for I myself am infinitely more important for you than anything I can give you — even than the most brilliant thoughts. So when thoughts do come, welcome them, and when they do not flow freely, simply rest back and love, and grant me the shared joy of being loved by you. For I, too, by my very nature, am hungry with an insatiable hunger for the love of all of you, just as your love reaches out at your highest moments to all the people about you.

So child, I, even I, God, whom people have foolishly feared and flattered for my gifts, I want love and friendship more than I want groveling subjects. So while we love each other, child, my share is as keen as yours.

He continues, "I have written in this letter what my tongue said as I let it speak, not because I wish to recommend any of the above as prophetic, but simply because I think it may prove helpful to those who have been dissatisfied with their own contact with God and who may find this a helpful practice in making contact with God."[1]

But another kind of dialogue is best written. For me the verbal dialogue of Laubach sometimes feels awkward and difficult, and I find written dialogue to be much simpler. My first instructor in writing dialogues was Ira Progoff. His method of writing makes use of techniques similar to those used in Gestalt therapy. Although I never attended a session with

1. Frank C. Laubach, *Letters by a Modern Mystic* (New York: Student Volunteer Movement, 1937), pp. 9-30.

61

Progoff, I got a copy of his book, *At a Journal Workshop,*[2] and I did each of the exercises he outlined. It took me the better part of a year to work through his journal-writing techniques, but it was worth it. I found them healing, integrative, and redemptive.

What I learned about dialogue writing has served me well in making entries in my journal — which, of course, is what Progoff intended. One way I have introduced this technique to participants in classes, workshops, and retreats has been through writing dialogues with Christ. After reading the story of the healing of the paralytic in the Gospel of Mark, I suggest that participants imagine they have been left alone with Jesus at his home in Capernaum. In his presence they are free to ask him any questions that come to them. After they write down their first question, they are to listen for the answer that comes to them, and then write it down. They carry on this dialogue until there is nothing left to say. Many persons have found this helpful in their conversation with Christ.

My interest in dialogue sensitized me in a particular way to its use by other Christians, especially writers. Recently I conducted a seminar on Carlo Carretto. While reading his books again, I clearly saw how he frequently engaged in dialogue with Christ. Here is an instance of Brother Carlo's dialogue from *The God Who Comes:*

> "Here is a summary of everything.
>
> "I can no longer say I am incapable of loving, because He replies to me, 'I gave you charity at Pentecost.'
>
> "I can no longer insist: 'What is charity for me, how can I get to know it,' because He will tell me, 'Do as I did. Love as I loved.'
>
> "And how did you love, Jesus?"
>
> "I loved by dying for you. You try, too, to die for your brother."
>
> "What does it mean, Jesus, to die for my brother? Must I, too, expect an end like yours?"
>
> "No, I don't believe so and I hope not, because, although it is good to die crucified, it is not good that there should be crucifiers. Now I shall explain what dying for your brother means. Listen! 'Love your enemies, do good to those who hate you' (Luke 6:27).
>
> " 'When someone slaps you on one cheek, turn and give him the other' (Luke 6:29).

2. Ira Progoff, *At a Journal Workshop: The Basic Text and Guide for Using the Intensive Journal* (New York: Dialogue House Library, 1975).

"'Be compassionate as your Father is compassionate' (Luke 6:36).

"'Do not judge. . . . Do not condemn. . . . Pardon . . .'" (Luke 6:37).

"Enough, Jesus, quite enough. I am in the habit of forgetting these words. I should like you to explain to me through a simple example."

"Well, read over the story of the prodigal son: I am the father who pardons."[3]

As I read this dialogue, it occurred to me that Carretto's books speak of God so deeply because he wrote them out of a profound consciousness of the presence of God. He sat before God, looked into God's face, conversed with God, and wrote the words that came to him. His writings are like journals of his communion with God.

The dialogical approach to God offers help not only to saints like Laubach and Carretto but to all of us — it fits into all of our lives. Like prayer or meditation, writing dialogues brings us into a deeper communion with the God before whom we live.

Prophetic Speech

God's self-communication has often come through prophetic utterances. God's words come to the servant of God, and they fill his or her mind with truth and images of new possibilities. The prophet is driven by a compelling urge to speak what God has revealed. Prophetic speech is human speech attributed to inspiration from God's Spirit. Most often it is prefaced with "Thus says the Lord. . . ." But with the prophet Miriam, Aaron's sister, it was a song, one she sang after the Lord had delivered Israel from Pharaoh. After they had passed through the Red Sea, Miriam took a tambourine in her hand, and all the women went out after her with tambourines, and they danced. "And Miriam sang to them, 'Sing to the LORD, for he has triumphed gloriously; horse and rider he has thrown into the sea'" (Exod. 15:21).

The prophet Samuel spoke these words: "Thus says the LORD, the God of Israel, 'I brought up Israel out of Egypt, and I rescued you from the hand of the Egyptians and from the hand of all the kingdoms that

3. Carlo Carretto, *The God Who Comes* (Maryknoll, N.Y.: Orbis Books, 1974), pp. 198-99.

were oppressing you.' But today you have rejected your God, who saves you from all your calamities and your distresses; and you have said, 'No! but set a king over us.' Now therefore present yourselves before the LORD by your tribes and by your clans" (1 Sam. 10:18-19).

Isaiah spoke his prophecy to the servants of King Hezekiah. When the servants of the king came to Isaiah, he said to them, "Say to your master, 'Thus says the LORD: Do not be afraid because of the words that you have heard, with which the servants of the king of Assyria have reviled me. I myself will put a spirit in him, so that he shall hear a rumor, and return to his own land; I will cause him to fall by the sword in his own land'" (Isa. 37:5-7).

Words of prophecy come in response to specific situations like the deliverance from Egypt, the unfaithfulness of the people, and the need for direction and assurance in the face of an uncertain future. Words inspired by the Lord, coming from the depths of the prophet's consciousness, expressed in his own frame of reference and through his own vocabulary. Prophecy reveals truth with power.

People today customarily dismiss the direct speech of God to human ears. Our fear of deception and delusion has made us rule out the continued speech of the God who spoke through Miriam, Samuel, and Isaiah. We reason, "Surely this God no longer speaks, and if the Lord does speak, it most certainly would not be to us." Yet I firmly believe that the prophetic spirit has not died, nor has it ceased to speak.

Because prophetic speech has not faded completely into oblivion, there are still prophets among us. I believe there are professors with whom I teach that are prophets; there are pastors of congregations who have the gift of prophecy; among the laity, gifts of prophecy often reveal themselves in committee meetings, classes, and private conversations. Living before God means listening for prophetic speech and being attentive to the word of God that comes to us through another.

This word of God may then come through our own lips. Sometimes we ask for this word from God; at other times the word comes to us of its own accord. It gives us assurance that we are to speak it.

This prophetic word can be heard in the writings of Brother Carlo. The prophetic speech never calls attention to itself; it blends into the text so smoothly that you would miss it if you weren't seriously looking for it. One instance of prophetic speech can be found in his book *The God Who Comes*. This message is ostensibly for Carlo, but as we read it, we are drawn into it and quickly realize that Carlo listens to God not for himself alone but for us also. God's message to him, therefore, becomes a prophetic message to us. Jesus speaks to Carlo:

"Before accepting your embrace I want proof of your fidelity.

"You are too sensual for Me to give Myself as food for your desires which are so poor in love, and so saturated with egoism.

"You believe you love Me, but in reality you are loving yourself.

"It is always the same!

"You must make some progress before leaving yourself and what is yours.

"For your sake I left what was mine and came to you.

"You do the same.

"Wait for me all your life as though I were coming every evening. I shall be present, and you will not see me; I shall be your lamp, and you will not realize it; I shall embrace you, and you will not feel anything.

"Then I shall know truly whether you love God because He is God, or whether you love Him because He is the solution to your problems. . . .

"Accept faith as it is — naked. Wait all your life for the God who is always coming and who does not show Himself to satisfy your curiosity, but unveils Himself before your faithfulness and your humility."[4]

Listening to godspeech would be a productive and creative way for teachers, preachers, and retreat leaders to prepare themselves. If we are not speaking God's word, whose word do we speak? If we are not intent upon re-presenting Christ, whom do we present? Once, when I was preparing to speak to four hundred ministers in Hershey, Pennsylvania, I asked the Lord what I should say. In the silence that followed, these words came to me:

Tell the men and women of God that I have not forsaken them, that I am with them in their struggles, in their pain and in the preaching of the word to my people. Say to them that the promises of God are true, that they can rest their lives upon what I have said to them.

Invite my servants to revisit their call. Tell them to come back to the sacred ground upon which they stood when I first spoke to them. If

4. Carretto, *The God Who Comes*, pp. 99-100, 101.

they stand there, listen, and open themselves to the call, it will echo in their ears again, and they can go from this conference with a deep sense that they are beginning anew with me in the power of the Spirit.

Talk with them about prayer — about entering into the closet of their souls and listening for me there. Tell them it is all right to write down what they think I am saying to them. I do speak through their minds and hearts. They often forget about that.

You may introduce them to deeper ways of prayer — to the silence, to images of my presence that sometimes fade, and to the certainty of my Spirit with them in the darkness of faith. It is in the dark that I am speaking and acting, but so many of my servants do not know that. They think that I am only with them in the light and in the jubilant times of their lives. Show them that I walk with them into their depths.

You might speak to them about "Lessons from Elijah's Cave." What does a man or woman learn in the darkness, in aloneness, in the midst of shaking and quaking? Speak to them about these things. This is what my servants need — to know that I am with them and working with them even in their darkness.

Do you not believe that hearing God's prophetic word would have an amazing impact upon our efforts to live before the Holy One? Not only does the challenge reach deep within the heart of every pastor, but it offers hope for all the baptized that they, too, are agents of the prophetic word. In the years to come, perhaps we will once again recognize the One before whom we live and let ourselves be open to the creative word that God wishes to speak through us.

Liturgical Speech

Living before God will be enhanced by listening not only to the Solitary Voice, the Dialogical Voice, and the Prophetic Voice, but also to the Liturgical Voice of God. God speaks through the liturgy in the corporate gathering of the congregation. Perhaps, as in no other way, this manner of godspeech offers an enduring way to ground us in God.

I first began to notice the divine Voice in liturgical speech through the reading of the Psalms. I commented to my colleague, Walter Brueggemann, that at the conclusion of a prayer or affirmation in a psalm, the Voice of God seemed to break forth. He explained to me that often after a

66

confession or a request to God from the people, the cantor or priest spoke the words of God. Psalm thirty-two offers an example. In the opening verses of the psalm, the writer declares how blessed are those whose sins are forgiven. He then confesses his own struggle with making confession of sin and the bodily consequences of withholding it. But he goes on to say how blessed he was when he did acknowledge his sins. Because of his own blessedness, he exhorts everyone to make a full confession of sin.

Listen to the exhortation of the psalmist: "Therefore let all who are faithful offer prayer to you; at a time of distress, the rush of mighty waters shall not reach them. You are a hiding place for me; you preserve me from trouble; you surround me with glad cries of deliverance" (Ps. 32:6-7).

Then comes the Voice of God: "I will instruct you and teach you the way you should go; I will counsel you with my eye upon you. Do not be like a horse or a mule, without understanding, whose temper must be curbed with bit and bridle, else it will not stay near you" (Ps. 32:8-9).

If, as Professor Brueggemann says, these are words spoken by the cantor or priest, can you imagine the power of these words when uttered to the congregation? The human voice of the priest becomes the voice of God.

But do we not have the same opportunity in each worship service to listen for the Voice of God through human voices? What occurs through the call to worship, or the words of forgiveness, or the benediction?

In an effort to place myself before God during worship, I listen for the divine Voice in its human form. For example, I listen carefully for an invitation from God in the call to worship, whether spoken or sung. My favorite call to worship comes from Psalm 100: "Enter his gates with thanksgiving, and his courts with praise. Give thanks to him, bless his name. For the LORD is good; his steadfast love endures forever, and his faithfulness to all generations" (vv. 4-5). I try to think of these words as the Lord's invitation to me to come before him.

After the confession of sin, when the minister speaks the words of assurance, I listen for the Voice of Christ saying to me once again, "Your sins are forgiven!" And as the service of worship closes, I listen for the blessing of God in the words of the benediction. During this final blessing, I open my arms to receive it from God, and at the conclusion of the benediction, I often fold my arms and hands over my chest to symbolically press it into my being.

All this may sound somewhat strange or even juvenile. But these rituals keep reminding me that all of my life is lived before God and that, through the liturgy of the Lord's Day, I am invited consciously into the presence, forgiven of my sins, and blessed to go forth and live joyously the life God has given me.

Conclusion

In this exploration of godspeech and the description of four modes in which we discern it, I hope that several things have begun to happen. I trust that you have been reassured that God does speak to us in our lives today. The attitude of expectancy helps open us to receive the truths God wishes to communicate to us. And I also hope that you see new possibilities in weekly worship and everyday occurrences to listen for God's word to you. Whether your communication is solitary speech, dialogical speech, prophetic speech, or liturgical speech, what matters most is that you are listening for the God who seeks your attention.

Questions for Reflection and Discussion

1. What are the similarities and differences between the four modes of godspeech?
2. Has there been a time in your life when God seemed to be communicating with you? What was it like? How did you respond to it?
3. How can other Christians help you to discern God's voice?
4. What is your greatest fear of listening to God?

A Journaling Exercise

1. What are the questions you have in your life today?
2. Choose one of these and write it at the top of a page in your journal. Or type it into your computer.
3. Sit quietly until possible responses to your questions begin to come into your mind. Record the ideas that come to you, maybe words God speaks to you.
4. Don't be too surprised at what happens!

CHAPTER SIX

Imagining God in an Ordinary Day

Driven by the conviction that life has depth and everything in our lives has meaning, we are compelled to look at the unfolding experiences of a typical day with expectant eyes and receptive hearts. The God who speaks, speaks in the ordinary events and interactions of the day. What excitement this adds to a routine day! When we renounce the flat world of sight and sense as the whole of reality, a new world of enchantment and mystery begins to be born. It's not that the material world is unreal, but it is incomplete. Neither is the enchanted world of spirit new; rather, we are reclaiming our organs of perception — eyes of the heart and ears of the soul — to notice what has been there all along. Perhaps our culture is finally waking up after centuries of sleep.

These new ways of perceiving the world enable us to experience more fully the meaning of our lives and to reflect more clearly upon the One before whom we live and move and have our being. This reflective engagement with the in-rushing material of everyday life not only draws us more deeply into an awareness of God but helps us to recognize the subtle but discernible acts of God in the ordinariness of our days. This vision of life, far from being new, is actually a return to the kind of vision that breathes through every page of the Bible, imbues the stories, teachings, and miracles of Jesus, and gives substance to our faith.

The depth of the world in which the drama of our lives is played out manifests itself in the ordinary things that we engage in every day. These repetitious things include getting up in the morning, dressing, eating, going to work, discharging our responsibilities, meeting and talking with a variety of individuals — and a thousand other occurrences in the course of a month or a year.

The depth of life operates beneath a thin guise in all these events, and all persons are close to it. The depth of life resides in the world but also within every individual, yet it goes unrecognized by many. While this spiritual depth is in all persons and in the ordinary happenings of the day, it is also beyond them, outside their reach or grasp. This mysterious depth has its source in the Spirit, an inexhaustible source of life, energy, and mystery. The divine mystery always stands beyond us yet continuously comes toward us, inviting our attention, showing itself to us, and drawing us into itself.

To hear God in the day requires us to break out of old habits and well-rehearsed rituals that are automatic. We must begin to see with new eyes and listen with new ears and imagine our lives differently! This sharpened attention provides the context for our continuous awakening to new dimensions of life and faith and God.

Some of us have difficulty waking up to this reality around and beyond us. Our lives have too often become so routinized that we are like bytes of data preprogrammed in the Cosmic Computer. An example comes from a conversation I had one day with the president of the seminary where I teach. While we were talking, he brought up the new signs featuring the college's name.

"Do you know what finally convinced me to put up these signs?" he asked. "These nice, new, brick-and-stone signs?"

"What?" I asked. And in response he told me an interesting story.

"I met a woman who asked what kind of work I did, and when I told her that I was the president of Columbia Seminary, she asked me where the school was.

"'On Columbia Drive,' I answered.

"'It is not,' she replied.

"'Well, I believe it is, because I've been going to work at that address every day for nearly ten years.'

"In amazement she responded, 'No. It couldn't be. I drive up that street to work daily. In fact, I've driven up that street every day for twenty-two years, and I've never seen Columbia Theological Seminary.'"

So we got new signs! How amazing that a school with millions of dollars' worth of buildings on fifty-four acres of land could be invisible to a person for over twenty years, especially when she drives by the site every day! The issue is awareness. She looked, but she did not see. Her seeing

70

had become so routinized that the landscape had become invisible. Perhaps some of us look but do not see because we have become habituated in our perception.

I trust that a few of the insights I share will sharpen your awareness and awaken your expectation that you will meet God in the ordinary day. What a glorious posture to assume toward life!

Seeing through Biblical Lenses

I have suggested that this world of depth breathes in the pages of Scripture and presents itself to us in the teaching and promises of Jesus. Numerous texts in the Older and Newer Testament suggest this deeper dimension of existence. Listen to the prayer of the psalmist:

> I keep *the LORD always before me;* because *he is at my right hand,* I shall not be moved. Therefore my heart is glad, and my soul rejoices; my body also rests secure. . . . *You show me the path of life. In your presence there is fullness of joy;* in your right hand are pleasures forevermore. (Ps. 16:8-9, 11, my italics)

The person offering this prayer has been touched by the mystery. She has looked into life and discovered it has depth. She knows the immediate presence of the Lord as One always before her, leading her. The Lord stands at her right hand as support and walks with her as a companion. Living with the certainty of the divine presence brings joy and gladness to her life. Only in this presence does she know fullness of joy. This person has been invited into the flow of the Spirit's power, and as she lives and moves in the Spirit of the Lord, she knows not only joy but fulfillment and surety as well. Unlike the woman who drove up Columbia Drive for twenty-two years without seeing the seminary, this person has her eyes open and her ears tuned to the music of another sphere.

This spiritual dimension of life stood at the center of Jesus' teaching. On the eve of his departure from the earth, Jesus promised his disciples, "I will not leave you orphaned; I am coming to you" (John 14:18). Orphans, children forsaken by their parents, are left to fend for themselves with no support or assurance. In his final hours on earth, Jesus promised his disciples that they would not be left alone, abandoned to

71

their fears. Rather, he said, "I am coming to you." He kept that promise. He came in the presence of the Spirit and remained among them.

This promise has never been exhausted: the One who gave his word to those waiting disciples came to them, and he still comes to his disciples today. The biblical revelation inspires the faith in us that God by his very nature is "the One who comes." Out of sheer grace, God came to us in the creation, in the words of Moses and the prophets, in Jesus Christ the Son, and in the Spirit. God takes the initiative to be with us; God is always coming.

Carlo Carretto captured this marvelous truth in words akin to poetry:

> God has always been coming. He came in the creation of light, and he came yet more in Adam. He came in Abraham but was to come more fully in Moses. He came in Elijah, but was to come even more fully in Jesus. The God who comes takes part in the procession of time. With history He localizes himself in the geography of the cosmos, in the consciousness of man, and in the Person of Christ. He has come and has yet to come.[1]

The God who comes makes a path into every day of our lives. The promised presence touches our lives through the continuous invasion of God into the world and into our days. This presence often becomes so palpable and so constant that we often ask with the psalmist,

> Where can I go from your spirit? Or where can I flee from your presence?
>
> If I ascend to heaven, you are there; if I make my bed in Sheol, you are there.
>
> If I take the wings of the morning and settle at the farthest limits of the sea, even there your hand shall lead me, and your right hand shall hold me fast.
>
> If I say, "Surely the darkness shall cover me, and the light around me become night," even the darkness is not dark to you; the night is as bright as the day, for darkness is as light to you.
>
> For it was you who formed my inward parts; you knit me together in my mother's womb. I praise you, for I am fearfully and wonderfully

1. Carlo Carretto, *The God Who Comes* (Maryknoll, N.Y.: Orbis Books, 1974), p. 1.

made. Wonderful are your works; that I know very well. My frame was not hidden from you, when I was being made in secret, intricately woven in the depths of the earth.

Your eyes beheld my unformed substance. In your book were written all the days that were formed for me, when none of them as yet existed. (Ps. 139:7-16)

For some, waking up to the presence of Christ in their everyday world comes with a jolt. The light blinds them. Can you imagine what it would be like to walk out of a dark closet into the light of the midday sun? Wouldn't the brilliance be too much for eyes accustomed to the darkness? The cloud of presence hanging low upon us all burdens some people beyond their ability to cope. One day as I was praying the Psalms, I discovered a request that shocked me. The psalmist actually asked the Lord to turn from him in another direction, to get away from his life, because the presence felt oppressive:

"Hear my prayer, O LORD, and give ear to my cry; do not hold your peace at my tears. For I am your passing guest, an alien, like all my forebears.

Turn your gaze away from me, that I may smile again, before I depart and am no more." (Ps. 39:12-13)

This seeker for God reveals another side of the presence. Sometimes God presses in upon us from all sides. God seemingly will not leave us alone. And, like this man or woman, we ask God to back off and give us space because the terrible presence of the Lord smites us with such awe that we cannot abide it.

The Coming of God in a Day

Where is God speaking, if not in this day? Where does God come to us, if not in our ordinary lives? And how does God come to us, if not through the things happening in our earthly existence? So, if we are to welcome the God who comes, we must learn to welcome all the events and experiences of the day and examine them for signs of God's presence!

The Bible gives witness to a God who enters into the world and participates in our history. Nothing happens to us apart from God. Numerous fleeting experiences have begun to convince us of the depth in life; sometimes we glimpse it, and sometimes we feel grasped by its power. Yet at other times we tend to believe these experiences are mere wishful thinking and thus ignore the subtle invitations to explore something more for our lives.

From time to time I have looked closely at the unfolding of my life, and on occasion I seemed to get hints of the Holy in an ordinary day. I've been aided in this project by persons like James Fowler[2] and Ira Progoff,[3] who have helped me look at large parts of my life. By examining the turning points in my life and the various chapters that emerged, I've been able to see my life in its wholeness. But other spiritual guides have suggested that I look at shorter portions of life, like a month or a week, even the unfolding events of a particular day. They have suggested that I divide the day into short sections according to what I was doing. By reflecting on these short segments, I could see not only how I was investing my time but also the signs of God's presence. This process has also proved to be illuminating. This examination of consciousness has made me aware of occurrences in both my inner and my outer world.

In light of my own discoveries, I recommend that you think of a day as the NOW, the time you will encounter God and interact with him. Divide this day of your life into brief episodes and write about them in paragraphs. Once you've described them in abbreviated form, muse over the day and give thanks for all that has happened. Always keep a kind attitude toward yourself, even when you fail. This act of separating your day into "pieces" and meditating on it makes you conscious of your unfolding life and postures you to see God's activity close at hand.

Attending to my life in this fashion, I've discovered two things to be enormously helpful — wondering and imagining. When I have segmented my day according to activities like getting out of bed, driving to work, keeping appointments, teaching classes, and other similar activities, I have found it beneficial to wonder about each event in my life. I wonder how God might have been in those events, and how the meaning of a day might be woven into the fabric of my ongoing story. Wondering does not require an answer. Yet sometimes an answer offers itself.

2. James Fowler, *Stages of Faith: The Psychology of Human Development and the Quest for Meaning* (San Francisco: Harper & Row, 1981).

3. Ira Progoff, *At a Journal Workshop: The Basic Text and Guide for Using the Intensive Journal* (New York: Dialogue House Library, 1975).

Imagining grows out of wondering. When I've wondered about the presence of God or the intention of God in something that has happened, my imagination often leaps from wondering to a strong conviction of the presence of God in that occurrence. This sense of the presence may come at the very time that I meet someone or get a phone call.

Frequently, when I've been talking with someone in my office, I've gotten the distinct impression that they were sent to me. I don't have that sense about everyone, but on occasion I'm gripped by the conviction that these persons are fulfilling an appointment not of my making or theirs — a divine appointment. In these instances I think the flat world of appointments and conversations is transformed into a meaningful world of divine encounter through a daring act of imagination.

Maybe a look at one of my ordinary days will illustrate more fully what I mean by encountering God in the unfolding of the day.

These events took place in my life on November 11, 1996, a random day I chose to examine as a bearer of the presence of God in my life. Here are the segments of the day that I identified:

- I woke up with a cold.
- I had my usual morning time with God.
- I ate breakfast.
- I spoke with my wife.
- I read the newspaper.
- I spent time thinking about the class my associate and I would teach.
- I went to work at about 11:00 A.M.; greeted my wife (who is my administrative assistant) and associate.
- I had lunch with the faculty.
- My associate taught the class on the passions.
- I kept an appointment with a former student.
- I had dinner, watched some TV, and went to bed.

Certainly there are many ways to reflect on the unfolding of this day. Here are several questions I found helpful in thinking about this day before God:

1. As I look back over this day, what was the flow of the events?
2. What hungers of the heart did I feel?
3. What questions grew out of my experience of life today?

4. Did anything puzzle me today?
5. Did I have moments that left me with a sense of the mystery of life?
6. Did I have any recurring thoughts?
7. Were there *kairos* moments, moments when I felt that God was presenting godself to me in a special way?
8. What was God doing in my ordinary life today?

You need not answer each of these questions about every day; use those that awaken you to "something more" in your day. If one of these questions triggers a chain of thought, stay with the flow of ideas until they've exhausted themselves. Use the questions to help you wonder about God in your life. Think of them as starters!

Suppose I take the last question — "What was God doing in my ordinary life today?" — and reveal to you the thoughts it inspired. My thoughts about God in my day followed this progression: Although I awoke with a stuffy nose and hoarseness, I discovered that the presence of Christ does not depend upon how I feel physically. During my time of waiting before God, I had a strong, mysterious sense of the presence even though my head was stuffy. Living in awareness is a gift that depends only upon my ability to receive it. After a time of living in awareness, the transformation of consciousness begins to occur. As this transformation occurs, I awake in the morning aware of another dimension that spontaneously presents itself. I seem to be living on two levels at once. Presence *is.* Living with openness to the Spirit makes me feel like I'm participating in the fullness of reality, both the physical and the spiritual simultaneously. Perhaps God in the events of this day showed me that the faithfulness of the presence depends not upon my feelings of well-being but upon the Other who always comes to me as a gift.

As I continued my prayer about this day, I wondered, *Is it presumptuous for me to seek to discern God's manner of speaking, to learn the vocabulary of the Spirit?* Something inside me spoke: *It is not presumptuous of you to wonder, to search in this dimension for my manner of speaking.*

I spoke to God: *You put the thought in my heart and the urge in my soul to learn your way of speaking. It is not for my own satisfaction that I seek to learn your way of communication. I do not look for a special place of honor. When I am quiet before you, you speak, but when I run throughout the day, I take away this opportunity for your Spirit to address me.*

My associate wanted to review our class for today. *Maybe you were in the concerns for our students that we shared before class. Meeting and talking*

76

about issues in the class provide an opportunity for me to mentor this servant of yours. She has so many gifts for ministry: she is a quick learner, a joy and a delight to work with, and a spiritual companion for many. With gratitude I receive this association as a gift from you.

At lunch I listened to one of my colleagues with whom I have long had an inner struggle. With a new pair of ears I heard him speak today. I think that I understand him and his strange behavior more fully. *As I reviewed this encounter, did you say to me that I am beginning to understand and accept him as a brother and fellow servant?* Maybe I don't need his recognition and approval in the same way I did sixteen years ago.

After lunch I conducted the first half of the class but taught poorly. After my associate made her presentation, I lectured about her lecture.

The class concluded with an interesting exercise. After my associate's presentation on the passions, I distributed paper plates and crayons to the students and asked them to use the crayons to symbolize their virtues on the inside of the paper plate and then to symbolize their vulnerable areas on the outside of the plate. When they concluded these two assignments, I asked them to write a letter of wise counsel to themselves. The idea of using the plate was good; it provided the students with a way of externalizing their feelings and fears. *I always think you are involved with me in acts of creativity like this. I have no idea where these ideas come from if not from you.*

When the class ended, I apologized to my associate for possibly having given the impression that her lecture was inadequate or that I needed to either correct or upstage her. I don't think the class got that impression, but they could have. She accepted my apology.

After class, when one of my former students came for a visit, it at first seemed like any other appointment. I liked Charles very much and had been instrumental in his coming to Columbia Seminary.

After graduation from seminary, for reasons neither of us was quite sure of, Charles had decided to take the Georgia bar exam and practice law part-time while he worked with men's groups under the auspices of a local church. He had made the appointment with me to bring me up to date.

Once we had greeted each other, he started explaining how this division of labor began making him feel increasingly tense. The law firm was intensifying its demands on him. He was seriously considering giving up his church work to practice law full-time. He wasn't quite sure what to do, but he knew he had to change something to lessen the tension in his life.

Just as his tension was peaking, the staff at the church where he worked held a retreat. Early on at the retreat, Charles announced his decision to practice law full-time as his vocation. Spontaneously, one of the staff asked, "Why not give up law and do ministry full-time?" The words struck him with such force that he couldn't let go of this notion.

When he returned home, he told his wife about the encounter. She quietly responded, "Why don't you do ministry full-time? I've supported your practicing law because I love you and I'm committed to being a helpful mate to you whatever you choose to do, but I'd really like to see you in the church full-time."

Still unsure about the direction of his life, Charles called an old law partner in Washington, who said, "Our firm in Atlanta is hiring. Why not apply for a position?" Charles did apply, but he prayed the interview would go badly. But before the firm could hire him, another incident occurred.

At worship the following Sunday, the minister closed his sermon by saying, "If you wish to join this church or talk with someone about giving yourself to the lordship of Jesus Christ, come forward." After the service, Charles went to the minister and spoke to him about giving his life over to the lordship of Jesus Christ. The minister was surprised because he knew Charles well, but he prayed with Charles. For Charles, the way became clear: he gave up a successful law practice to work for the church full-time.

When Charles completed this long story of joy and struggle, he said to me, "I wanted you to know about this because you've played an important part in my call to the ministry. I still recall the day that you became part of my story. You asked the group in the workshop I was in to identify with one of the persons in the healing of the paralytic, and I chose the paralytic. I realized that I was on the mat and needed to be taken to Jesus. That experience has become a key to my life and ministry. Often I ask a group of men, 'Who is on the mat today?'"

"God has brought you full circle," I said to Charles. "Nothing is ever wasted."

What a gift this random appointment turned out to be! I had no expectations other than finishing another day and going home. But the hour held so much more than I had anticipated. Here was a gift from God, an insight into faithful living, and a sense of the divine presence working through human speech.

As I think back over this day, it stands in sharp contrast to those bland, shallow, unexamined days when I rushed through the hours from one task to another without considering that I am always living before God.

Other Ways, Other Days

Not every day unfolds as smoothly as the one I chose to reflect on. Sometimes the day holds pain and disappointment or things so trivial they seem worthless to you or to anyone else. Yet, in living faithfully in these flat days and living them before God, we become transformed persons and please God. Every day is a gift from God, and who are we to complain about the content of a particular day?

Jean-Pierre de Caussade says, "To achieve the height of holiness, people must realize that all they count as trivial and worthless is what can make them holy. . . . Consider your life and you will see it consists of countless trifling actions. Yet God is quite satisfied with them, too."[4] This lesson on "throwaway" experiences can help us greatly if we remember that nothing is wasted, no life is useless, and no actions are trivial when we embrace them as bearers of God's will for us.

To deal honestly with God through the everyday happenings of life, we must accept the painful as well as the fulfilling moments, because both give life richness. Some days seem to be one long, continuous trial: we offend someone we love, we yield to the temptation to think evil of another, we resent the person who falsely accuses us, and we suffer disillusionment when reality shatters our dreams and hopes. These draining experiences come to everyone, whether they live deeply or in the shallows; they are part of being human and living in a world like ours.

I have had days when life did not flow smoothly, when a day's events shattered my dreams and shook my world. I vividly recall one particular episode with several days like that. It began with a disappointing meeting with a friend at breakfast. I had discussed with him the idea of underwriting a program I was developing at the seminary. My goal was to make pilgrimages to Israel part of this program — a goal that seemed to further his dream of giving others the opportunity to visit the Holy Land. For several months I had been laboring under the impression that he was responsive to my request. Quite suddenly it became obvious to me that we were viewing the funding from very different perspectives. At that point I asked for a breakfast meeting to discuss the situation.

The discussion verified my fears; we were indeed at different places. I took responsibility for the misunderstanding and apologized. My friend

---

4. Jean-Pierre de Caussade, *Abandonment to Divine Providence,* trans. John Beevers (Garden City, N.Y.: Image Books, 1975), p. 15.

79

both heard and accepted my apology. I suggested that we begin our conversations again to see what we could work out.

Subsequently I made a different funding proposal to him regarding the program and asked him to consider it. He said that he would. When the day came for the decision, his answer was "No." I felt that his response put me in an embarrassing situation. I had made plans and had made promises to registrants, and now I didn't have adequate funding. But this friend also came to my rescue. Although he said "No" to funding the whole program, he made a generous offer to fund those who were presently registered in the program. I was indeed grateful for this bailout.

My reaction to this particular day surprised me. I could have been more disappointed, depressed, and self-condemnatory. My mixture of feelings suggested to me that there was more to this experience than a mix-up in communication. I reflected on the pieces of this puzzle and wondered what the Lord was saying to me through the fear and confusion I had experienced. The following thoughts came to me.

First, working with my friend on his dream enabled me to see how a pilgrimage to Israel could change the way a minister reads the Bible. If I had not made several pilgrimages to Israel (the first of which included my friend and his wife), it would never have occurred to me to make the pilgrimage part of the program I was developing.

But I think the Lord, through the painful miscommunication about this endeavor, was trying to tell me something — not that these pilgrimages weren't important, but that I shouldn't place quite so much emphasis on them in my own work: *I have not called you to make pilgrimages the center of your ministry. Care for my leaders, both clergy and lay. Teach them. Be a friend to them.*

It also occurred to me that having a single sponsor for the program could create an unhealthy dependency. Too much dependency, and the loss of freedom it implies, could place me in an uncomfortable position. Having worked through these feelings and possibilities, I began to see that other options might be available. In fact, the very next week a travel agent visited me and told me about special fares for ministers who were making pilgrimages to Israel. These fares, which included all expenses, were quite reasonable, and there was sufficient funding built into the program to cover them.

Ultimately, my response to this experience is one of gratitude. I am grateful for a friend who came to my rescue and stood by me at a crucial moment. But I am also grateful for his decision not to provide complete funding for my project. I must say honestly that when I was in a dark and fearful place, not knowing how I would make good on my promises, it was not easy for me to see God in my disillusionment. But with the crisis behind me, I am grateful for God's acting in ways that I did not understand.

In addition to both ordinary days and painful days, there are some days that seem to be punctuated with *kairos* moments, moments when ordinary time is suspended or transcended, and another kind of time invades our consciousness. These momentary invasions come spontaneously, without warning, freezing rationality and opening us up to a different way of knowing. These strange and wonderful moments are like gifts; they leave us with a sense of both joy and grace.

As I review the years, I recall several of these moments of grace that defined my life. My first experience of this suspension of time came when I was seventeen years old. It was the night that the living Christ presented himself to me. Another moment came during the first evening I met my wife, a "too good to be true" moment. Then there was a moment a few years later when a word came out of the darkness while I was on retreat at the Monastery of the Holy Spirit: *You are a servant of the Lord in waiting!* And the confluence of finishing my Ph.D. degree, wanting to teach in a theological seminary, and meeting an old friend at the mall who chaired a search committee for a professor of evangelism and church growth produced yet another of those moments.

As I review these episodic moments, they seem to have come at crisis points in my life. When I have been confused about my identity, felt a deep longing for fulfillment and companionship, questioned my vocation and sense of call, or when I have come to the end of my strength and have not known how to proceed, God seemed to come with gracious assurance. These special moments often brought clarity, encouragement, and empowerment. I don't recall having asked for any of them.

One of these special moments occurred when I met with the travel agent I just mentioned. An appointment with a travel agent doesn't sound like material for the creation of a *kairos* moment, does it? Yet this man held the solution to the major problem I was struggling with. On this ordinary day, this man presented me with an extraordinary offer. When he finished his presentation, it was as though I had been visited by an angel. I felt an urge to jump up and hug him.

I restrained my body but not my mind. For the moment my normal mode of thought was suspended and a feeling of "I can't believe what I'm hearing" took over. This feeling of joy, mingled with relief, arose deep down inside of me. For an hour my heart glowed with gratitude. And, as I reflected on my visit with the agent, I saw the Spirit of God in a way that never occurred to him. To me it was a serendipitous gift of God that liberated me to continue an important ministry.

I could say that this man was an angel to me — angel does mean "messenger of God." I do believe that on some special days, angels do visit us as God's messengers. Don't ask me more about this idea, because confessing a scant faith in the visitation of angels is about as far as I can go. A brief statement in the letter to the Hebrews does bolster my faith: "Do not neglect to show hospitality to strangers, for by doing that some have entertained angels without knowing it" (Heb. 13:2).

Look at Your Day

I have no idea why it took me so long to begin listening for God in the unfolding events of a day. Maybe it was ignorance. Or maybe I got caught in the routine of programmed living. Another possibility was fear, pure and simple. Was I for a long time afraid that I wouldn't see anything, or see anything good, or afraid that making these connections with God was an illusion that wouldn't stand the test of time? Whatever kept me from recollecting the day has been set aside, and I'm grateful that I often meet God in the hours of unspectacular days.

This serious work of looking for God in the unfolding of our lives gives incarnational substance to faith. When we name and contemplate the things that happen to us, a conviction of the presence and activity of God begins to form in our consciousness. This transformed awareness turns into expectancy, so that each new day finds us full of anticipation that some common, ordinary bush will be burning and will signal us to pull off our shoes because we are standing on holy ground.

When we have lived long with a consciousness of God, the expectation of the presence begins to be woven into the warp and woof of our souls. The signs of presence just beneath the surface of the natural, the ordinary, and the expected will appear when we pause to listen. Suddenly we begin to hear the sounds of another land. We discover a vaster, more sublime language that communicates meaning. Best of all, we come to know that the sounds we hear are a mere echo of the true and lasting sound, and the perceptions we have are images of the invisible, hidden in the unfolding day.

Imagine how different your life will be — living in dialogue with the One before whom you live today and forever!

Questions for Reflection and Discussion

1. What does Psalm 139 teach us about the presence of God?

2. What hinders our noticing God in an ordinary day?

3. How does the Incarnation of God in Christ serve as a paradigm for our viewing the day?

4. Recall and describe an incident of God's coming in your day.

A Journaling Exercise

1. In brief paragraphs, record the events of yesterday.

2. Read over the list slowly and reflectively.

3. Give thanks for the specific content of your life yesterday.

4. Once again, review the day and wonder where God was present in your ordinary day.

5. Write a letter of thanks to God for the presence that was in your life yesterday.

CHAPTER SEVEN

Coming to the Present

Where is the God before whom we live? If we search the geography of the cosmos, I doubt that we will find the dwelling place of the Most High. There is no mountain high enough or ocean deep enough or expanse large enough to contain God. The God before whom we live cannot be somewhere because the living God fills everywhere.

If we search for the divine in the eons of time, we confront another impossibility. Looking for God in the past in archaeological ruins or stories of ancient people, at best we discover only the footprints of God on the beaches of time, but we don't localize God in a particular time. If we imagine the place of the Holy One in the future, in a million billion years, we will not find God in the future, though we might imagine the faithfulness of God who guarantees time. If we should conclude that God cannot be found in the past or discovered in the future, we might suspect our failure points to God's habitation of eternity, but eternity seems far too vast for us to grasp, too mysterious for us to picture.

Perhaps this excursion into space and time abolishes all hope of meeting God except in the present, in this moment of consciousness. This present moment, I believe, defines the time in which we meet God; the place in which we stand defines the place of divine-human encounter. Our meeting with God is here and now! The Lord God does not meet us in the past, which, once lived, becomes history that dies and is buried in archaeological ruins and a faulty memory. Although God holds the future and guarantees it through grace and faithfulness, it has not yet been born in human awareness. The God of the future exists by anticipation only.

I wonder if these staggering thoughts gripped the mind of Thomas Kelly when he wrote about the "Eternal Now" as the possibility of experiencing the divine presence as a repeatedly realized and present fact:

> Once we discover this glorious secret, this new dimension of life, . . . we no longer live merely in time but we live also in the Eternal. The world of time is no longer the sole reality of which we are aware. A second Reality hovers, quickens, quivers, stirs, energizes us, breaks in upon us and in love embraces us, together with all things, within Himself. We live our lives at two levels simultaneously, the level of time and the level of the Timeless. They form one sequence, with a fluctuating border between them. Sometimes the glorious Eternal is in the ascendancy, but still we are aware of our daily temporal routine. Sometimes the clouds settle low and we are chiefly in the world of time, yet we are haunted by a smaller sense of Presence, in the margin of consciousness.[1]

Living before God occurs in the present, in which the past is a memory, often faded like an old shirt, and the future is an expectation, like the sun rising tomorrow. Even though memory and intuition call forth the past and imagine the future, neither of these creative capacities can help us experience God anywhere but now. Now we can awaken to the presence. Now we can attend the Holy One. And, when in the present moment we do awaken and give our attention to the God before whom we live, eternity invades time, transforming the moment into a God-moment, a segment of holy history.

What is the posture for this bold expectation? Perhaps to contemplate God in the present, we need to be constantly alert to our tendencies to run toward the future or retreat into the past. Does this mean we need to be sentries on guard?

Biblical Reflections

The time of our lives, the time we have to live before the Creator and Lord, is a gift every moment. These moments combine to make seconds, minutes, and hours until a day is born. The psalmist, seeing this union of

---

1. Thomas Kelly, *A Testament of Devotion* (New York: Harper, 1941), pp. 67-68.

the segments of time, exclaimed, "This is the day that the Lord has made; let us rejoice and be glad in it" (Ps. 118:24). This day — not yesterday, because it is now history, and not tomorrow, because it exists only as possibility — this day is the one the Lord has made.

One morning I was thinking about the moments of a day, and it seemed to me that I had a vision of the birth of the present moment: it was like watching the birth of time. I was thinking about living in the present moment and how I could escape from my preoccupation with the future and come to the present. In my contemplation the image of a fountain in the bed of a canyon came to me, and for a moment it seemed I was looking over the rim of this vast canyon, which opened up the source of being where time had gestated and now was being born. I could see every moment coming into being, one after the other. As time was coming into being, I realized that it was time for me and for everyone. Seeing the birth of time made me deeply aware that all of us share in one thing — the present moment. Every person, every nation, everything in nature all share in time, in this moment of time. The birth of each moment makes it possible for us to be and to be together in God's gift of the moment. I am joined with everything through my participation in the present moment.

Everything flows out of the fountain of time; the surging waters bring forth all that exists. Grace, being, providence, love, and energy flow from the fountain. Without time, none of them would come into being.

And in the birth of the moment I am one with all things everywhere, regardless of the time of day. It may be night for me and day for another, yet it is the same time — this moment. This is indeed the day God makes, moment after moment after moment.

Without time, nothing has being, not one single thing. Jesus taught us that each of these moments bears God's love to us. In this particular moment God enters into the world, becoming the shield of our lives and opening our consciousness to the divine presence. In a simple but powerful way, Jesus urged his followers not to concern themselves with the future, especially with possible catastrophes and losses. In the present moment our heavenly Father watches over us, provides for us, and offers us fellowship with the Eternal. Recall how Jesus expressed this gracious presence in the present:

> "Therefore I tell you, do not worry about your life, what you will eat or what you will drink, or about your body, what you will wear. Is not life more than food, and the body more than clothing? Look at the

birds of the air; they neither sow nor reap nor gather into barns, and yet your heavenly Father feeds them. Are you not of more value than they? And can any of you by worrying add a single hour to your span of life?" (Matt. 6:25-27)

Do not worry about your life! A negatively imagined future produces worry. I learned long ago that the presence of God cannot be experienced as future. This does not deny God's presence in the future, but it reaffirms that we can experience the presence only here and now.

I have, at times, found myself worrying about catastrophes in the future — poor health, insufficient resources for crises, the possibility of failure. In my misspent energy in constructing these negative possibilities, I have never experienced the assistance of God's grace. On the other hand, when my father died at age fifty-four, when my mother lost her faculties to old age, when my children had to undergo surgery or face other kinds of danger, God was present in the moment to give courage and strength.

If today is the day of graciousness, if today God comes to us and provides for us, we should learn to respond to God's presence now. But we are so prone to forget, to ignore the signs of the presence and the voice that speaks to us. With this in mind, the writer of the letter to the Hebrews recalled a time when Israel did not attend the word from God. For forty years they wandered in the wilderness, accusing, disobeying, and provoking God's anger. Finally God declared to the chosen people that none of them would inherit the land promised long ago to Abraham.

Urging us to pay closer attention to God in our day, the writer says, "Therefore, as the Holy Spirit says, 'Today, if you hear his voice, do not harden your hearts as in the rebellion, as on the day of testing in the wilderness. . . .' But exhort one another every day, as long as it is called 'today,' so that none of you may be hardened by the deceitfulness of sin" (Heb. 3:7-8, 13).

I have sought various ways to attend the moment, to become mindful in the present. On my visits to the Monastery of the Holy Spirit, I occasionally ask the abbot, Bernard Johnson, to give me spiritual guidance. He is a faithful follower of our Lord and sensitive to the ways of the Spirit. One day I asked him, "How can I live faithfully each day before God? What help can you give me in being alert to the Spirit?"

The first suggestion he gave me was from an old novice master, perhaps the one who had introduced him to the way of monastic life. He said, "Believe that everything that happens in your life happens for your good or God's glory. But you must take everything in this light, for one denial breaks everything down."

Most days this is not too difficult — but then there are the other days. We have difficulty on those days when we feel betrayed, when calamity befalls us, when our way turns dark and gloomy. The old novice master, intent on helping the young novice keep to the course, added, "One denial breaks everything down." Would taking everything that happens to me as being for my good or God's glory help me live more faithfully in the present?

Then the abbot suggested that I pray the Serenity Prayer daily: "God give me the grace to accept the things I cannot change, the power to change the things I can, and the wisdom to know the difference."

Finally, he encouraged me to adopt the attitude of Teresa of Ávila, a sixteenth-century saint who founded a Holy Order and developed a deep, spiritual friendship with Saint John of the Cross. According to the abbot, Teresa said that we all need two senses: a sense of faith and a sense of humor. If we wake up without a sense of faith, then we must lean on our sense of humor. If we awake without a sense of humor, then we must lean on our sense of faith. Accepting every aspect of life, regularly praying for such acceptance, and developing the two senses we most need will keep us joyously in the present.

To live before God requires us to live fully in the present moment. The text of the Newer Testament affirms its importance, the teachings of Jesus encourage it, and the wisdom of the abbot gives practical advice for doing it. What would it be like for us to accept everything as happening for our good or for God's glory? How would we be affected by praying the Serenity Prayer every day? How would we be changed if we lived by a sense of faith and a sense of humor?

A Reflection on Present and Pre-sent

Consider a few aspects of what it means to be present to the existent moment. To be present means to be at home in your body: where your body is, there you are, not somewhere else. To be present means to be here in this moment of time and not lost in the past. To be present means that you resist running to the future for greater anticipated fulfillment or deeper anxiety and that you choose to focus your awareness on this instant. To be present in this second means to be aware of your surroundings, what is taking place, and how it all connects with you. Being present means to be recollected.

To come to the present means to come to this present moment, the one in which you now have your being. Coming to the present means being present to the present.

I think it's interesting that the noun "present" is spelled exactly like the verb "present," in which the accent shifts from the first to the second syllable. These two words that are spelled alike are quite suggestive for the challenge of living in the present moment. If we think of God as the one who presents the present, then we might receive it as a present, a gift. To present means

"to make a gift to" — the present moment is a gift from God.

"to bring into the presence of another" — God presents this moment to us as challenge and opportunity!

"to offer for consideration" — God is asking us to consider what is happening in us and to us in this moment. Each moment offers an opportunity for decision or re-decision.

"to portray as a character on the stage" — God presents himself in the guise of the events of our lives, inviting our discernment.

Our Father presents to us each and every moment, moments born in the womb of time, which come to us freely, to be embraced and filled with meaning. In this role, the Most High comes to us as a servant offering a gift, a role so clearly modeled when Jesus took the basin of water and the towel. When God presents these moments to us, they offer a wonderful freedom that gives us space to reflect and decide on our response. The events of our lives present us with many guises and disguises in which the living God appears before us. On the stages of our lives this gracious God indirectly confronts us with new and amazing revelations of godself.

What insight into living in the present moment would we gain by thinking not of God as the presenter but of ourselves as the presenters? What if in every moment of our lives we endeavored to present our lives to God? What would that mean to us? To God?

If in every moment we were "to make a gift of ourselves to God," we would be recognizing that we are not our own but belong to God. Paul had this in mind when he wrote to the Romans, "I appeal to you therefore, brothers and sisters, by the mercies of God, to present your bodies as a living sacrifice, holy and acceptable to God, which is your spiritual worship. Do not be conformed to this world, but be transformed by the re-

newing of your minds, so that you may discern what is the will of God —
what is good and acceptable and perfect" (Rom. 12:1-2).

In each moment that we present ourselves to God, we are like the
newborn that the nurse brings to her mother for the very first look. The
birth of each new moment gives birth to a new person who presents herself to God.

When we come repeatedly into the presence of God, we issue an un-
spoken request for God's consideration of our lives. Not only does God's
consideration of us lead to correction and change, but God's knowledge
of our love and devotion surely gives God pleasure and delight.

We are indeed actors on the stage of history, playing out a part. Not
all the events of this drama are worth preserving in the memory of God:
crime, war, and abuse illustrate the kinds of things not worth saving. But
the children of God who wear the family crest and who moment by moment live their lives before God share in the creation of a history that will
endure forever in the memory of God.

To Come to the Present Moment

Coming to the present can become a habit that pays rich dividends. Yet
these riches cannot be distributed by reading or thinking alone. We must
actually *come to the present* to know what it means.

When we *come to the present,* there is a new creation, and a whole
new world is born. The world that appeared so lifeless and meaningless
takes on breath and feeling that enliven every part of it. We might say that
it becomes enchanted.

Regarding this amazing transformation, Carlo Carretto says,

> "I don't know how it happened to you, but I know how it happened
> to me.
>
> God arrived in my heart like a huge parable. Everything around me
> spoke to me of Him.
>
> The sky spoke to me of Him, the earth spoke to me of Him, the sea
> spoke to me of Him.
>
> He was the secret hidden in all things, visible and invisible.
>
> He was like the solution to all problems.
>
> He was like the most important Person who had ever entered my life
> and with whom I should have lived forever.

Very soon I felt myself enveloped by Him as a 'Presence always Present,' one who looked at me from all the leaves of the wood I was walking through, and across the clouds riding briskly along the sky above my head."[2]

When we *come to the present,* we are rescued from all worry and anxiety about the future. The future has not come yet, its experiences have not unfolded before us, and there is little to worry about when we are living in the present.

Had I known that my apartment would burn during my first year of seminary, I would have been extremely fearful and anxious. God does not give grace to comfort imaginary ills. But when sufficient reason for fear and anxiety came through the loss of everything that my family and I owned, I wasn't anxious. In that particular moment my fears were calmed by the grace of God.

When we *come to the present,* there is no grief or remorse to deal with. When we have faced our past with its sin, failure, and shame, and have released it to God, there is nothing to worry about in the past; it is gone. So when our minds wander back to some painful part of our past, we simply "come to the present" and leave the old memories alone to die.

All of us have experienced painful misunderstandings. A miscommunication I once had with a person I admire and respect affected me deeply. He had assumed that the project we had agreed upon would be funded by his foundation and that he would later be reimbursed for the cost. This central assumption was never spelled out. When I received a letter requesting the return of the capital, I was shocked and angry, then depressed.

I thought about the issue for an entire weekend. Voices in my head were alternately arguing, judging, and explaining. This inner dialogue continued far longer than I care to write about. Finally I broke the cycle and came to my senses. I came to the present moment. The new dialogue I had with myself helped me:

Can I do anything to correct this situation today? No.
Is my friend accusing me? No.
Are there reasons for me to feel mean, diminished, or a failure? No.

2. Carlo Carretto, *The God Who Comes* (Maryknoll, N.Y.: Orbis Books, 1974), p. 153.

Then come to the present and be responsive to what is before you, not what you imagine!

When we *come to the present,* we experience reality. What is real is now; what is real is here; what is real is the experience of the moment. Reality is here before us, being presented to us by God, and our part is to present ourselves to him!

Another experience also gave me cause to come to the present. I was lecturing to a church group one day when I suddenly felt overcome by my ineptness in leading the group. I was devoting the morning to speaking about the spiritual journey and prayer. After giving out energy for a couple of hours, I began to feel depressed. The voices in my head told me that I was of no value, unappreciated, and ineffective. The more I thought about the bland experience I was having, the more depressed I got.

The voices continued for the rest of the morning, even invading my thoughts at lunch. In the midst of my self-pity, I remembered that God was to be found not in the hours that had passed but here at the lunch table, now, in my new situation. Then I "came to the present." There were no voices speaking in the present; nothing was wrong in the present moment. When I stopped believing the lies my mind had invented and imagining the criticisms of others, I lost my feelings of depression and inadequacy. I realized that I could survive if I was not valued by these people — and furthermore, that I didn't even *know* what these people thought and felt about me.

In this moment I gave myself to God. God appreciated me. I was pleased for God to do whatever he would with me. This was reality, and this was what was happening in the present moment!

When we *come to the present,* we experience grace. Grace is not given to quell our anxious imaginings about the unknown future. It is not given to assist our rumbling into the past, rooting up some old feeling of self-pity or condemnation. Grace is given in the present moment to help us deal with what stands before us.

I remember the time I was leading a retreat in North Carolina. After one of the sessions, a woman came up to talk with me about her experience of God, or the lack of it. She was feeling far from God. How could she feel close to God as she once had? "When I go to the mountains and look at the peaks," she told me, "I feel the majesty of God and sense the nearness of God's presence. But when I get back to the flatland, the sense of God seems to evaporate. What can I do?"

"Come to the present," I said to her. "At this instant, God for you is not in the mountains or in the flatland. God is in the present moment. If you can believe it, you are in the presence of God this very moment! Don't look for God to come in the way you experienced in the mountains. Look for God to come as he is, as he chooses to come in the present moment."

Then I added, "Perhaps God is speaking the language of absence. Maybe you need to learn this new dialect of the Spirit to hear God in your present moment."

In *the present moment* we tap meaning, being created in the matrix of the presenting God, the presenting self, in the present moment. The meaning of the moment escapes us if we aren't paying attention, if we don't accept the actuality of what is happening to us — including dark days and sleepless nights. Most of us fear these dark times in our lives, thinking that God has forsaken us.

Jean-Pierre de Caussade says that there is nothing safer and less likely to lead us astray than the darkness of faith. The very darkness can become our guide. How can this be? Can you hear this as grace? Can you believe that God is in the "darkness" as your friend and guide? The psalmist says, "My companion is the darkness . . ." (Ps. 88:12).

What I'm suggesting is that these feelings of abandonment during our journey open us to God's presence in a new form. Think about it for a moment: Does not the darkness of faith mean that we walk in a blinding light?

Realizing these things and accepting them helps us come to the present. And when we do this, we stop wasting great amounts of energy trying to reconstruct and change our lives rather than let them be.

When we *come to the present,* we are grateful! How can we not feel gratitude? We see, feel, and experience the present world of a presenting God. We have life and being and possibility, and in the moment when that dawns upon us, praise and gratitude are spontaneous offerings of our grateful souls.

Perhaps my invitation will mean more to you now when I say this:

Come to the present; it is
    . . . the time that you have
    . . . the place of your life
    . . . the place of God's grace.
Come to the present; it is
    . . . all that you have
    . . . all that matters
    . . . where all obedience begins.

Come to the present:
    The Place of God.

So we must learn to live in the present moment. The present moment is always the presenting moment — God presents godself to us, and we present ourselves to God!

A Psalm

God, as I sit before you and
ponder,
I realize your presence
now.
I am being seen by you
now.
I need not look for you;
I need only to let myself be seen.

Life in you is in the
present.
Healing from you is in the
preset.
Power to overcome is in the
present.
Worship and service are in the
present.

Equip my mind with the armor to protect the
present:
Faith, to shield my imagination from
either fear or regret;
Truth, to pave the pathway
of my mind;
Righteousness of life, to protect
my heart;
The Sword of the Spirit, to slay my
doubts;
And prayer always as the air I
breathe.

Questions for Reflection and Discussion

1. What does it mean to "come to the present"?

2. In what ways does "coming to the present" characterize the life of Jesus?

3. What seems to keep us from "coming to the present"?

4. What happens to you when you "come to the present"?

A Journaling Exercise

1. Find a quiet place for your journaling.

2. Come to quietness and stillness. When you are still inside, complete each of the following sentences in a short paragraph:

"In the present moment, my world consists of . . ."

"In the present moment, I am thinking about . . ."

"In the present moment, I am feeling . . ."

"In the present moment, God is . . ."

CHAPTER EIGHT

Acknowledging God in My Heart

Practically speaking, how do we place God in our prayer? Where is God? This simple, childlike question may evoke an easy answer: "Everywhere!" Truly, God is everywhere and in everything, but how can we pray to "everywhere"? How do we think of "everywhere"? If we are to engage God in prayer, everywhere must be somewhere. To pray to a God who inhabits everywhere would fragment our consciousness and splinter our prayers even more than the distractions they already suffer.

A review of my stages of prayer will perhaps offer you a variety of postures, but they eventually lead to God in my heart. In my first efforts at prayer, I placed God on the rim of the universe, looking at me from afar and, I hoped, listening to me. Thinking of God as "up there and out there" kept the presence far, far away; the relation took the form of a long-distance phone call in which I did most of the talking. When I offered intercessory prayer, it seemed like I was persuading — or trying to persuade — God to be good and get involved with those persons for whom I was praying.

Eventually praying to God on the rim of the universe gave way to praying to God closer at hand — even in the room with me. I recall this radical shift as one that introduced me to talking with Jesus as if he were sitting in a chair in front of me. To add to the concreteness of the encounter with him, I even placed an empty chair before me in which I imagined him sitting. For a time, praying to the Christ seated before me gave focus and clarity to my prayer, but eventually this image became too fixed. What had begun with spontaneity and a deep sense of reality became frozen, rigid, and controlled. Eventually "Christ sitting before me" became a technique, and methods, no matter how well-intentioned, are short-lived in vital prayer.

As time went on, praying to Jesus in the chair seemed to make him into an idol. I do not judge those who have found this imaginative way of praying helpful. For some it does not lead to idolatry, nor do they use this envisioning of Christ as a means to manipulate God. It can truly be a helpful way to pray, but neither this nor any form endures.

To avoid the perversions of prayer before Jesus, I sought out a different perspective on the place of God in prayer. Following Nicholas of Cusa, John Donne said, "Our seeing God is not so much our seeing as being seen." An amazing shift in consciousness occurs when we let ourselves be seen rather than trying to see. I found myself being set free from images of any sort, and the thought of a person before me soon became the thought of a presence behind me. When I conceived of God as behind me, the presence was out of my line of vision, and an image was not required. Being seen required having an awareness of God's presence, not possessing a mental image of God. Quickly the image changed to presence, and I experienced prayer as being before Another whose face I could not see and did not need to see.

Being seen felt so easy. I didn't struggle to focus on Another, only to be before this One who saw me, knew me, and loved me. My attention was not passive and indifferent but open, active, and receptive. My effort changed from seeking God to letting myself be found by God, from focusing my eyes to see to letting myself be seen. Being seen by the "everywhere" God shifted the effort from imagining God in all places to conceiving the divine presence in this place.

Notice in this narrative how, over the years, I have envisioned God moving closer and closer to me. My adolescent efforts at prayer were directed to a God who dwelt in outer space, somewhere up, out, and beyond me. Then the distant God became a presence in Christ before me. This move from "God out there" to One before me with whom I spoke made communion and fellowship possible. The God from Beyond may break into consciousness in episodic moments to issue commands or effect a spiritual transformation, but these moments occur infrequently and leave us wondering when the next visitation may occur.

The shift from God before me to God behind me came late in my spiritual development. With that relocation I lost the need for images (how can you image what you cannot see?), and the previous forms of Jesus before me changed to a presence around me. God, whom I do not see, is with me as presence. God loves me, knows me, and presents godself to me, but I do not see God — God sees me. Yet, in faith, I see God seeing me.

At this late stage in my life, I am struggling with yet another transition: God in me. The idea, of course, is not a new one. Since the early days of my discipleship, I have been aware of his promise to be with us and in us. I have known for years the texts that speak of his being the Vine, and I one of the branches, and of my being baptized into his body. There is a vast difference, however, between knowing the texts and experiencing them.

I have come to believe that God teaches us when we are prepared to learn and leads us when we are able to follow. This notion of spiritual readiness has led me to the conviction that it is Christ who teaches us to live before God. As the Master Teacher, he finds a way to direct us at the appropriate time into the next steps for our lives. Knowing something of his manner of speaking made me notice and pay attention to an idea that kept coming to me in my prayer. Repeatedly, in the silence, these words came to me: "I am in you. Attend me in your heart." For more than three years this direction persisted: "Think of me as being in you."

The Struggle

Do you understand why it would be such a struggle for me to believe that God is "in me"? I am not worthy to house the holy presence. God surely has servants who are more effective than I am. Why did God choose to speak with me about being in me at this time of my life? After I had struggled with the presence being in me for a few years, I asked the Lord what I should do. I wrote down what I thought God said:

> Be content with my call upon your life. I have chosen you from the beginning to be in the family. You have been given the gifts that you need to do the work that I wish you to do. Fret not because you lack the disciplines, the looks, the knowledge, and the experience of many others. All your life has been prologue for this moment in time, and you will be ready for what I choose for you to do.
>
> Pay attention to what I am trying to teach you about my presence. As I have said to you during this past year, "I am in you. My Spirit is nearer to you than you are aware. Even in your sharpest moments of

awareness, you do not recognize how near I am to you." Learn to relax and to trust that I am at work in you, in your searching, in your finding, in your dreaming. Notice. You have gifts that others do not have, even as they have gifts you do not possess. Be content with your own gifts. Whether you recognize them or not, your gifts are considerable. Others see them more clearly than you do.

Try to remember me during this year! I am with you, whatever happens to you. I will be in it with you to make good come out of it.

In these words, which came to me at the beginning of a new year, God was encouraging me to believe what he had been impressing upon me repeatedly during the preceding year. I found sufficient encouragement and strength to take a small step toward believing that the presence was actually within me.

Perhaps one other illustration will make it clear how the Lord has spoken with me about the presence being in me. I find myself recalling the reality of "him in me" more often, but it is still hard for me to grasp or be grasped by this truth:

In teaching, preaching, and consulting with my children, all you need do is remember that I am in you. I have chosen you, you have been baptized into me, you have been long in the process of appropriating the meaning of your baptism, and this is as it should be.

When I am in you, speaking and leading through you, you need not struggle or strain. I will speak through you and work through you. Remember what your doctoral class said to you yesterday: "You have been the most help to us in this supervised ministry by listening to what we said, being engaged with us, and then thinking about what to say. Watching your face and the expressions on your face while you were thinking about what to say taught us much."

What they experienced when they said these words was the presence of my Spirit in you, giving you discernment.

During this year I will teach you more about resting in me. Keep the image of the vine and the branches before you. I am the vine; you are one of the branches. I am in you, and you are connected to me. My life in you will bear fruit.

Some days when I enter into my prayer time, I do have a sense that the Spirit of God is in me. This awareness doesn't lead me to images of

God but gives me a clear sense of being present to the presence. One day when this happened, I felt an urge to write a prayer of response:

> Today when I came to pray, I had a sense that you were right here with me, that you were noticing me today. Your voice came to me without asking. You said, "I am not only with you; I am in you. When you suffer, I suffer with you; when you are afraid, I give you courage; and I want you to look to me as you live into the next years of your life. I will be here, guiding you."
>
> You are the Lord, the grantor of mercy. I look for your mercy to be with and upon me today. I do not know if I have heard your voice accurately, but I believe you have told me to slow down, to take no more work for the year, and to cancel appointments that I do not need to keep.
>
> I thank you for your mercy. I know that you are with me and that you are working for the good of your name. Keep me in your will. Protect my mind. Cleanse my thoughts. Be near to me and make me into the person you have always seen me to be. Show me your priorities for me today and the days that are ahead of me. You are the Lord, the grantor of mercy!

These examples of my dealings with Christ's leadership in my developing life of faith may not portray accurately the depth of struggle I have experienced. I hope that they at least show the kinds of conversations I have had with God; these are merely illustrative of the many we have had over these last few years.

In my struggle to believe that Christ is in me, I have found an image from Paul Tillich helpful. He speaks of God as the Ground of Being, the ground of all being.[1] This notion shifted my vision of God from the heavens or the rim of the universe to the ground beneath my feet. Also, if God is the Ground of Being, everything that does exist, exists in and for God. This common foundation revealed how dependent upon God I am for all things, including my very being. But this vision of God also made it clear that I am connected to everything in the universe, because everything is grounded in God. This way of looking at the relation of creation to the Creator has opened my eyes to the God in me who is the God in nature, in all situa-

---

1. Paul Tillich, *Systematic Theology*, vol. 1 (Chicago: University of Chicago Press, 1951), pp. 112-58.

tions, and in all persons. Maybe it is possible for this Ground of my being to impart to me a consciousness of its presence within.

In addition to Tillich, James C. Fenhagen, former Dean of General Theological Seminary in New York City, has opened new ways of imagining God in my heart. In a deceptively simple little book called *More than Wanderers,* he states, "There is within each one of us a reservoir of spiritual energy that comes out of the very depths of our lives. It is like a deep well that we can draw from forever — a well that never runs dry. Its source is the love of God. Its vehicle, the Christ who dwells in us. . . . When we are in touch with his presence within us, it has a way of pulling us deeper. And as the rhythm of moving inward and outward is established, prayer is experienced as a beckoning from within."[2] This witness helped me realize that I have been engaged with the One who has been drawing me deeper and deeper into the source of life and energy. Fenhagen's deep well, the reservoir of the love of God, just may be the way into the Ground of Being, the fathomless depth of the divine mystery. And Fenhagen claims that this spiritual depth draws us into itself so that we may move outward, expressing the Holy in the ordinary experiences of life.

For me this concept gained further credibility when I came across a quote by Thomas Merton, the well-known Trappist monk of the Abbey of Gethsemani in Kentucky. He describes the divine/human connecting point in the depths of the human spirit: "There exists some point at which I can meet God in a real and experimental contact with His infinite actuality. This is the place of God, His sanctuary — it is the point where my contingent being depends upon His love. Within myself is a metaphorical apex of existence at which I am held in being by my Creator."[3]

Tillich uses "ground" as a metaphor for the divine presence, and Fenhagen understands this deeper dimension of existence as the love of God made real to us in Christ. Merton suggests that the finite human spirit possesses a point at which it encounters the infinite divine Spirit. These metaphors point to an intimacy with God that I am acknowledging as "God in my heart."

I haven't finished the struggle; it is with me daily. But I've committed myself to follow the guidance being given me in recognizing the pres-

2. James C. Fenhagen, *More than Wanderers: Spiritual Disciplines for Christian Ministry* (New York: Seabury Press, 1981), p. 32.

3. Thomas Merton, cited by Fenhagen in *More than Wanderers,* p. 32.

ence within. I am but a beginner on the pathway. My steps seem awkward and stumbling, and I proceed with many questions.

As I considered my novice role, it occurred to me that I might engage the Lord in conversation about those texts that speak so clearly of his presence within to see what might be revealed to me. I chose four significant texts to help me listen.

Promise of Presence

I asked Christ to explain to me what his presence in me meant. Here is the first instructional text I chose:

> "They who have my commandments and keep them are those who love me; and those who love me will be loved by my Father, and I will love them and reveal myself to them." Judas (not Iscariot) said to him, "Lord, how is it that you will reveal yourself to us, and not to the world?" Jesus answered him, "Those who love me will keep my word, and my Father will love them, and we will come to them and make our home with them." (John 14:21-23)

This is what I thought I heard Christ say to me:

> It is true. I did promise, "Those who have my commandments and keep them are the ones who love me, and I will love them and will manifest myself to them, and my Father will love them, and we will come into them and will make our home in them." What more can I say?
>
> In every way I endeavored to make my followers know my intentions to continue my life and work in them. I told them that I would not leave them as orphans, like a parent who runs away from responsibility or one who dies far too soon. Unlike the parent who leaves prematurely, I promised to come back to my followers after my death. They did not understand then, and my disciples still do not understand even now when I say, "I will come to you."
>
> I have been keeping my promise for two millennia — I came, I come, I am always coming. I am presence. I am present to you today just as I was present with my disciples in Galilee, even as I was present in visible bodily form after rising from death. I am still among you.

103

It has been a long time, and now you are becoming weary with wait-ing. Too often you think it was a wonderful idea, and it makes for an enticing memory, but you do not believe that I am here with you in your midst. My whole church has suffered much and long under the influence of the Enlightenment, and I am now ready to break its grip and liberate the imagination of my servants to see me here, now, to know me as I am in power and in love.

I said, "On that day you will know that I am in my Father and you in me and I in you." The day to which I refer is the day of my coming. I came first in the womb of a virgin; I came back from the tomb; I came to my followers in the Upper Room at Pentecost, filling them with a sense of my presence. On that day they knew that the Spirit was I my-self, and they realized in their own consciousness that I was with them in a way that I had never been with them before. I was *with them and in them,* transforming their human powers and manifesting myself through them.

Yes, on that day they knew that my Father was in me and I in them and they in me. The promise was fulfilled, and the mystery enshrouded them as it did on the Sacred Mountain. But it is important for you to-day to remember that this coming at Pentecost was not the last coming. I still come to my community when it gathers to pray and waits to re-ceive my presence. I still cause them to know that I am in my Father and he in me; I still show them that I am in them and they are in me. This is my promise to my people, good for all time.

When you keep the commandment of love, do you know how much you are loved in return? I love you, and my Father loves you. I prom-ised to show myself to you when you love in this manner. I do! I reveal myself to you through your acts of love, through your deeds of compas-sion, through your willing acts of forgiveness. The very spirit of com-passion with which you act reveals my Spirit. Just think — would you be that loving and gracious if left to your own inclinations?

And this is not all. I come to you in very special ways to make myself known to you. I show you how I speak with my people today; I will teach you my language.

Even more than promising to reveal myself to you, I promised, "Those who love me will keep my word, and my Father will love them, and we will come into them and make our home among them." I promised, and I do not lie. Love me, and my Father will love you. In the Spirit my Father and I come into loving hearts and loving communities; we settle down in them not as tourists who come and go but as holy presence that remains.

In a day when so many feel isolated and alienated, I long for them to know that I am with them. They do not realize the subtle, freedom-preserving initiatives that I take, seeking their attention. Even those who have been baptized in my name, who share in me, have been so mesmerized with this world's goods that they do not notice. So many of them still live in unawareness.

And my deepest pain is the poor members of my church who go on reading my words and confessing their faith but never giving me their attention. They have substituted their devotion to the church as a building or an institution for their devotion to me. They have turned aside; they have found other gods, more immediate and accessible. When will they remember that I am their foundation? I am their life, and apart from me they can do nothing.

I am present to them, offering myself to them, but they reject me, the Living Presence, in favor of a memory, a burned-out memory. I see them living on a memory of a memory when the Reality is at hand! I am pained. Sometimes I still weep!

The Hope of Glory

Here is a second significant text, another text of Saint Paul, which speaks of Christ in us:

> I became its [the church's] servant according to God's commission that was given to me for you, to make the word of God fully known, the mystery that has been hidden throughout the ages and generations but has now been revealed to his saints. To them God chose to make known how great among the Gentiles are the riches of the glory of this mystery, which is Christ in you, the hope of glory. (Col. 1:25-27)

". . . Christ in you, the hope of glory." What does it mean for you to be "in me?"

"In you" does not mean that I become part of you by a fusion of the divine and the human. For me to be in you means that I am in your awareness, that you think of me. Then at times I think of me through you. When you think of me, I am in your consciousness. Do you understand that this is not a fusion of my being with your being but a relationship, a connection? Just as when you are away from home and you think of your spouse, she is in your consciousness.

But to be in you is more than that. Being in your awareness defines the initial relationship, but "in you" also means that I am in your way of thinking. When you must make a decision or choose a course of action, I am there with you in the thinking, evaluating, and choosing. You might say that I am in your reasoning because the way you reason with my being in you is very different from the way you reason when I am not influencing you. You can always discover a depth dimension in each of the choices you make, choices that reflect my will.

When it comes to evaluation and judging or discerning, the ground of discernment is in me, and all the issues of your life pass for review before the presence of my Spirit. That is what it means for me to be in you, that I am a part of your evaluating, discerning, the way that you should go or the act that you should embrace.

The mystery of my being in you is greatest with respect to your choices. You are free because I made you that way, so that you share finitely in the freedom of my Father. Yet, even in your choosing, I am in your choices, guiding you and empowering you by my Spirit. When you choose my will, it is always with freedom, but it is my will you are choosing and not your own.

What does it mean that you being in me is my hope of glory?

First of all, you must remember that you have been made in the image of God, my Father. You have been made like him and for him. Anything less than the will, presence, and fullness of my Father will not be to your glory, will not give you the hope of glory.

Glory, you should know, is being like God, fulfilling the purpose of God for you, and this means overcoming the parts of you that contradict the image, purpose, and purity of my Father.

Your glory is not achievement, recognition, or power as the world thinks about it; your glory is the ultimate fulfillment of your being, which is at the same time the fulfillment of my Father's will.

My being in you as presence encourages your faith. My presence gives you confidence that you will come to the fulfillment of your life. Yes, this is glory, the inexpressible, eternal becoming of my Father.

106

The Temple of God

The third significant text comes from 2 Corinthians: "We are the temple of the living God; as God said, 'I will live in them and walk among them, and I will be their God, and they shall be my people. . . . I will be your father, and you shall be my sons and daughters, says the Lord Almighty" (2 Cor. 6:16, 18). Becoming the temple, the dwelling place of God — how could the intimacy of the human with the divine be greater? Was Paul beside himself with joy when he called us the temple of God? How should I understand it?

You are indeed the temple of God. Just as the ancient temple was erected as the dwelling place of my Father on earth, so I created the church to be a dwelling place of God on earth. This temple is constructed with living stones. My presence in you is always drawing you into a communion with other followers of mine who are living stones in the temple, the dwelling place of God.

Today, as then, people misunderstand the temple: they become devotees of the temple rather than devotees of the One whose temple it is. The religious persons of my day made so much of the place, the rituals, and the times of gathering, even profiting off the work of the temple, that they lost sight of the temple as his house. All the stones in the temple were cold and dead; no spirit lived in them — so much like the people that worshipped there.

My Father had hoped that in moving the temple from one sacred place to many sacred places, the people would understand that it is not the physical temple that holds his interest but the temple of the Spirit, the community of persons who, as the true stones, form the temple.

I wish my followers could understand how my Father aims to realize his purpose by drawing ever nearer to them. The original vision of "walking in the garden in the cool of the day" was rejected; the mighty acts of my Father have been intended to restore that sense of "living in" and "walking among" the chosen people.

The temple, which you call church, has been created by my Father as the new dwelling place of the presence. The church does not choose this grounding for its life. It is given. It simply is! The church is the temple grounded in the Mystery of the Holy One, my Father. Each manifestation of this "temple of God," each particular congregation must decide whether to rest in its ground and become what it is destined to be, or deny its essence and become perverted.

My Father will never force any community to recognize the presence and the ground beneath it. The Holy One values their freedom too much. My Father respects the creation too deeply to force the divine presence and will upon the community. Abba is there, always there, waiting.

My Father desires this earthly family to recognize their true foundations, to accept their vocation as children of God in exile, and to live as strangers and pilgrims on the earth, looking for a better land. The better land is a new country where my Father is everything to them, and they are fulfilled in his presence.

Now, as you know, is the time my Father has chosen to manifest the presence in new and transformative ways. Communities that welcome the presence become light to a darkened world; they become salt and leaven in everything they touch.

So, to be the temple of God means that as a community you house the divine presence. And what is true of the whole is true of each of the parts.

The Indwelling Christ

The fourth significant text is again from Paul: "I pray that, according to the riches of his glory, he may grant that you may be strengthened in your inner being with power through his Spirit, and that Christ may dwell in your hearts through faith" (Eph. 3:16-17).

What do you say about the prayer of your servant Paul?

I heard the prayer of my servant Paul, so long ago now. He prayed it because of my Spirit in his mind and heart. After all, I promised to come to you, to live with you and to make a home in you, and he was asking for only what I had promised. When you ask for what I have promised, you may be assured of my response. Truly, my servant Paul prayed for what I longed to give the baptized in Ephesus and in every place.

I give the Spirit to strengthen the faith and love of my followers. The gift of the Spirit is not so much a wind that blows from without as it is an eruption of energy from within. My Spirit in the deeper consciousness of persons reminds them of my faithfulness; the Spirit persuades them to keep holding steady when the way is hard; and when they speak for me, the Spirit infuses their words with conviction that persuades the listener of their truth. Do not try to live for me in your own power; it can't be done. Look to the presence of the Spirit within you to strengthen you and empower you for service and for the daily battles of life. When you ask for this assistance, I will give it.

I hear the request from the sincere soul who prays for my indwelling. As I promised, I will come into you when you ask. My coming will not be some flash in the pan but a settling down, a permanent presence, an indwelling friend.

I have but one purpose for coming into you and remaining as constant presence — to teach you to love. You do not know love apart from me; loving is what I teach. I do not make a recluse of you, because you learn love only in relationships. You learn love in all the places that your ego can become deflated by the actions of another, in relationships when you are slighted or misunderstood, in disappointment, and in conflict. I do not expect you to learn how to love instantly; it is a lifelong assignment.

Your perspective on love will change as you begin to acknowledge my presence in you. I will show you the length of love, how it has its beginning in eternity in the heart of the Father, and like an unbroken thread weaves its way through the unfolding story of history; and it stretches into the future until the future has dissolved into eternity before you.

I will help you to see that no one is excluded from my love. The love that I share with the Father embraces all races and all religions; it embraces the violent and abusive, the murderers, prostitutes, deceivers, and liars; my love embraces gay and lesbian persons and those who fear and hate them. Make the list. No one is excluded from the embrace of divine love. You do not yet believe this because you have not let yourself be loved with the fullness of this world-embracing love.

You will see that this love has a depth that reaches to the bottom of hell. In the days between my crucifixion and resurrection, I went there to announce liberation to the oppressed. All the disobedient, the demonic forces, and the Adversary himself had to hear of the love of the Father. My Father longs for all persons to be saved and to come to the knowledge of the truth. There is no greater love than the love that embraces its enemies.

Yes, the height of this love reaches to the highest heaven, to the heart of God. I know this love because I came to earth through its power. After the Father had made all things through me, and the creation went awry, I saw the anguish of perfect love, and that love being in me and part of me compelled me freely to come and reveal it to the world. I showed it to the world, but the world could not tolerate it. They tried to kill it, and in their failure they established it forever. The love that radiated from the cross is etched in the unconscious depths of the whole human race.

Only a few of my servants through the ages have glimpsed the depth of divine love. When they approached this abyss of passionate fire, they lost the power of reason and the faculty of speech, and in the darkness of faith they plunged into the ever-flowing fountain of divine love. Consumed by the Father's love, they were ruined for anything else.

Yes, I want you to be filled with this love because it is the fullness of God. Do not be astounded that I have such a rich desire for you. Let your poor mind rest a moment to comprehend what I am saying: "I want you to be filled with the fullness of God. It is not enough for you to have the presence in you; it must fill you."

Even my servant Paul had difficulty believing what I inspired him to write, and while he was struggling with the vision of being filled with the fullness of God, I whispered in his ear, "My Father can do exceedingly, abundantly, above all that you can think or imagine." This is also my encouragement to you.

Can you imagine what it would be for the fullness of God to fill you? Can you think such a noble thought? If you cannot birth so profound a thought, sit in the presence of my desire until the thought can take shape — be filled with the fullness of God.

If, finally, you cannot imagine the fullness of God, ask for it! Perhaps your imagination will be fired by the experience of it. Ask for it now.

My Father is able to *do all* that you ask or imagine!

My Father can *do more than* you can ask or imagine.

My Father can *do abundantly, above all* that you ask or imagine.

My Father can *do exceedingly, abundantly, above all* that you ask or imagine!

You asked what it means for me to live in your heart? All of the above.

Attending to God in Your Heart

I think Brother Carlo wrote his books listening to God. Though he doesn't always quote the conversation, his words come to me with such penetrating power that they must have been spoken through him by the living Christ. On some occasions Carlo slips: he puts the dialogue in clear print for us to see. One of those hints I found in *The God Who Comes:*

> "Jesus, it is so good to hear you speaking; speak to me again!"
>
> "What do you want me to tell you?"
>
> "You gave me the law of love, your love, and you made me understand that you are the law, you are the holy gospel, you are the way to love.
>
> "Help me, Jesus, to trace your footsteps. It is so difficult! Don't leave me alone!"
>
> "Why do you say to me, 'Don't leave me alone'? I never leave you alone; I cannot, since I am within you."
>
> "It seems like a set phrase, Jesus — 'You within me,' one of the rhetorical phrases which we use. But does it correspond to the truth, the whole truth?
>
> "Are you truly, effectively within me?
>
> "What mystery is in your words, Jesus!"
>
> "Yes, brother, I am within you.
>
> "What would have been the use of my death, offered for love of you all, if not to carry out the reality of this union of ours?
>
> "I died in order to overcome separation and to establish a kingdom in which whoever wants to be with me is with me."[4]

Perhaps Paul also had his own difficulties believing that Christ really did live in him, that he lived in him continuously, transforming his life into love.

As I move beyond the initial struggle with the notion of "God in me," I am discovering a kind of comfort. With my anxiety assuaged by his promise to be in me, to dwell in me, I can, on occasion, become quiet before his presence. I feel no need to speak, only to recall his promise: "We will make our home in you." Yes, some days I can actually believe that I

---

4. Carlo Carretto, *The God Who Comes* (Maryknoll, N.Y.: Orbis Books, 1974), pp. 205-6.

am the temple of God and that the whole faith community is the dwelling place of God. In gentle but persistent ways, Christ teaches me to rely on the presence, to trust him to work in me and through me as he wills.

Of all the contemplative postures we have explored, acknowledging God in my heart remains the most challenging. In spite of my stumbling efforts to recollect that "he is in me, and I in him," he keeps giving me grace and instructing me one day at a time.

A student recently told me about her relationship with a homeless person. When she confessed her pain to him, he touched her temple and prayed for her. Then he told her his daily prayer: "O God, this is your day, and I am your child. Show me the way." Perhaps this street person's prayer makes the vision much simpler than all the words I have written.

Questions for Reflection and Discussion

1. What does the phrase "acknowledging God in my heart" mean to you?

2. Review the four texts that speak of God being in us and explore again what these texts mean for you.

3. What anxiety do you feel about asking God to be in you? What delight?

4. What difference would it make in our lives, our churches, and our world if we acknowledged the presence of God in one another?

A Journaling Exercise

1. Write down this question: "Lord God, do you live in me?"

2. Wait five minutes in silence, stilling your heart and listening.

3. Write the words that come from your deeper self. Don't think or edit your intuitions. Let the words flow!

CHAPTER NINE

Celebrating Life in Freedom

When it came to writing on this theme, I suddenly felt confused and terribly ignorant. Why did I ever think about writing on freedom? What do I know about freedom, anyway? To get unstuck from my feelings of inadequacy, I asked the Lord, "Why did you put it into my mind to write about 'the freedom of the Christian'?" The answer came to me as I listened:

> I want you to write about freedom through my presence because so many who believe in me still bear a heavy load of guilty fear and shame. They are shackled by both concerns about past failures and fears of the future. I want them to know me as a "liberating presence," not as an oppressor.
>
> Despite all I have done through my Son, it seems that my creatures can never get the message: I am Freedom, and I desire their freedom. I want you to write about freedom for my people because at this moment you know more about freedom than you think. You have fought hard battles to learn that I am love and that I come to you as a freeing presence.
>
> Share your faith. Share your love. Share your freedom, and your witness will be heard as a welcome, liberating Word!

As I share these insights into freedom in the Spirit, I do not invite you to a sitting or standing posture. I invite you to dance. Dancing before the Lord! What a concrete metaphor of our freedom in Christ.

The Bitter Dregs of Bondage

This response to my inquiry led me first to reflect on the bondage I have known. To understand and appreciate freedom, we need to know what we have been set free from and what we are free for. So, to fully appreciate a life of freedom before God, I sought to name the bondage I have known for so long. A number of pictures revealing my own lack of freedom came to my mind.

I have known the bondage of fear that arises in a world without God. In my childhood I had no religious background or training. My parents were good people, but in my early years they weren't devoted church members. As I lived through those early years, I had fears of monsters in the darkness beyond my awareness. I was also an insecure child afraid to spend the night away from my mother. These fears and anxieties were intensified by the angst of which Luther wrote so powerfully. I had no shelter to protect me from the chaos, and I lived in fear. The bondage of fear didn't go away until I came to know the unmerited love of God. I thought that childhood fears were something that only I experienced until the day I heard professor James Fowler speak of "the terrors of childhood." At that moment I recognized that others had also been gripped by childhood terror! This terror held me in bondage throughout my childhood and adolescence.

I have known the servitude of dependency. My habit of looking to another for security began with an exaggerated reliance on my mother. When I was about twelve years old, I recall thinking about her dying and how lost I would be without her protection, understanding, and support. Those deep feelings of helplessness made me dependent on her complete approval. I easily became obedient to her out of the fear of losing her love. Throughout my adolescence my fear of abandonment controlled many of my choices and kept me imprisoned.

This dependency on my mother led to my being captive to other significant persons. A pattern of life formed in those early years that stretched into adulthood, making me a slave to the acceptance and affirmation of peers and authority figures. A continuous search for acceptance and approval held sway for the first forty or fifty years of my life. In order to get this approval — or at least think I was getting it — I suppressed my own feelings and conformed to the expectations of others. Can you imagine the bondage of making most of your decisions based on what you think others think of you?

I have known the bondage of forbidden knowledge and the bitter

114

fruit of shame. When I was ten years old, an older friend told me about the female menstrual cycle. The information seemed innocent enough, but it had a paralyzing effect on my ten-year-old mind. I had learned something that it seemed I wasn't supposed to know. In biblical imagery, I had eaten the forbidden fruit. Along with the fear of having profaned the sacred, I experienced a sense of shame because I possessed forbidden, secret knowledge. This sense of wrong burdened me for four or five years, and I didn't know how to find relief. The only response I could figure out was to turn away from the knowledge and pretend I didn't have it. And, as you would suspect, the harder I tried to un-know, the more fixed the knowledge became in my mind. Learning the forbidden secrets of life left me with a deep sense of shame, a bitter enemy of freedom.

I have also known the enslavement of guilt through breaking the commandments. Even though my mother and father were not strongly religious — not in the sense of going to church or having prayer in our home — they both were moral people who taught me right from wrong. When I broke one of the rules they had established, I felt guilty. For example, in the fourth grade I used my jackknife to carve my initials on my desk at school. The teacher took my knife away and kept it.

A few days later my mother asked, "Where is your knife?"

"At school," I answered.

My mother had talked with my teacher, who was also my cousin, and knew the whole story. So she asked if I was certain my knife was at school. At this point I told her the truth about my abuse of school property and admitted the lie. I don't recall the punishment I received, but I do recall how guilty I felt about lying to my mother. Guilt disrupts our consciousness and destroys our freedom.

In my teen years I experienced captivity to the law. The law, as it impacted my life, took the form of things you did and things you didn't do if you professed to be a Christian. I learned those rules from the Christian community in which I worshipped and from the mentors whom I followed. Not knowing the depth and extent of God's grace, I lived under the illusion that God's love depended upon my obedience. I often feared that if I broke the law of God, I would be expelled from God's family. Years later I learned that freedom was not achieved by performance; it had to be given by another.

I have experienced subjugation to success. On the surface it appears that success leads to freedom. But think about it. You have done what you most wanted to do; you have gained recognition and approval. Wouldn't you think that this achievement would free you from needing to succeed more and more? On the surface a glowing success may appear to be liberating, but in actuality every success calls for a larger success. The ego-driven voice within says to the invisible audience of imaginary admirers, "If you think that was great, wait until you see my next success!"

For many years I have struggled with my addiction to food. Persons with a food addiction get up from one meal thinking about the next. Patterns of eating between meals, especially after work and after dinner, add up to one or two extra meals a day. Soon the free man or woman in Christ becomes a slave to food. Slavery to lips, mouth, tongue, and taste buds controls food intake, weight, and health.

Obviously, when I think about freedom in Christ, I see it in relation to those peculiar forms of bondage that have oppressed me. I have come to believe that this persistent longing for freedom can be met only through the gift of God's grace. Through the life, death, and resurrection of Jesus, God has not only revealed the depth of suffering love but also shown us the breadth of it. Nothing short of unconditional love liberates us from bondage to ourselves, our fears, and the oppressive religious and cultural bondage everywhere present. I can know true freedom only through Jesus Christ.

What Do I Mean by Freedom?

Freedom is the capacity to evaluate options, to make choices, and to discover and act upon your deepest desires. Freedom also defines a state of existence in which oppressive forces do not control your destiny. Yet, if freedom does not include an ease and a confidence in the presence of God, it will soon dry up like a puddle of water evaporating in the summer sun.

Freedom means to reside within yourself, to accept who you are. To live true to your identity, employing the gifts you have been given, results in freedom. But none of these forms of freedom touch the God-dimension of life. How can anyone who lives with a sense of guilt for past sins and failures be free? How can anyone who is mired in shame be free? And there can be no freedom until the specter of death has been dealt with, and what human being can cast out the fear of death?

Truly free persons have come to grips with themselves; they know who they are and have embraced their unique being; they have recognized their gifts and use them with appreciation; they have discovered their place in life and claim it with gladness and humility. Centered persons like these face the same external pressures as everyone else — they know the distrac-

116

tions of a consumer society, they feel job pressures, they care about their duties to family and friends. Yet they are not enslaved by these external forces. And these free persons know a relationship with God that assures them of acceptance; they experience the grace of God as the neutralizer of shame. And eternal life, a unique gift from God, frees the children of God from the agonizing fear of death. Can you imagine this kind of freedom? Free to be yourself, free in spite of your circumstance, free from your own accusing heart, and free from your fear of the future. Is this not true freedom?

On a day still fresh in my memory, I met with a man who had known the bitter bondage of fear coupled with his artful manipulation. But now he was free, free to be himself. When my friend Greg requested a meeting with me, I had no idea what he wanted to talk about. After we spent half an hour speaking about things that had happened during the past year, the conversation took a sudden, serious turn.

Greg said, "It seems to me that our relationship progressed well to a point, but I recall a day when we began to separate from each other." As soon as he made the statement, I, too, had a vivid memory of that day. He explained how we had been competing to achieve conflicting visions and how the competition had driven a wedge between us. He stated clearly and convincingly that he both needed and desired my friendship. I was a bit stunned by his forthrightness, but I knew we could make no progress in our relationship until we bridged the separation.

I offered my perception of the alienating day. "I don't think I was competing over a different vision. I recall feeling manipulated and controlled, and I have a strong aversion to both. Perhaps I still have control issues in my life, but what I perceived as your efforts to take control of the situation made me suspicious. And I must confess to you that I was angry when we competed for one particular friendship we have in common."

Candidly, Greg confessed to me, "I've been doing some serious work with a counselor who has helped me see that I am a manipulator. When I behave in this fashion, people don't know where I'm coming from and suspect the worst."

Suddenly this man's frankness and vulnerability put me at ease and convinced me of his sincerity. If he didn't need to defend himself, I didn't need to suspect him of ulterior motives. In his newfound freedom he had become transparent in his dealings with me. And his freedom set me free to relate to him openly and honestly, without fear.

The conversation concluded with our thanking God for our encounter that morning and our reconciliation with each other. Jesus said,

"You shall know the truth, and the truth shall set you free." Truly, both of us had been set free. Freedom begets freedom.

As I look at the fear and suspicion in our world, I'm not surprised that homes are plagued with abuse. Understandably, racial tensions mount in an atmosphere of mistrust. Close relationships sour and break apart when confidence turns into suspicion. When these breaks occur, no one can be totally free.

But what if we had the kind of courage Greg displayed? What if we admitted our wrongs to each other? Wouldn't such candor open the way for trusting relationships that would set us free? What a different world we would have if we could find the path to freedom!

Freedom, Not License

I am writing about Christian freedom, which contrasts sharply with license. License, a misguided notion of freedom, assumes that persons can follow their own inclinations and impulses and do whatever they please without considering social norms or the rights of others. To remain free, everyone must choose in ways that respect the value of others and their right to be free. If my exercise of freedom places another in bondage, it is not Christian freedom that I experience.

In a treatise called *Christian Liberty*, Martin Luther said,

A Christian is a perfectly free lord of all, subject to none.

A Christian is a perfectly dutiful servant of all, subject to all.[1]

Luther understands Christian freedom to mean that we have been set free from all external means of gaining God's love. A relationship with God depends not upon our works or efforts of any kind but upon grace alone, faith alone. "For by grace you have been saved through faith, and this is not your own doing; it is the gift of God" (Eph. 2:8-9). To us who believe, freedom comes not through our own efforts to be good or holy persons but through the gracious act of God.

Yet Luther says that the Christian is also the servant of all. He creates a paradox by claiming perfect freedom through grace and complete service to others out of the gratitude that freedom engenders. Freedom through faith in Christ originates in grace, and servitude to everyone made in God's image springs from grateful hearts.

1. Martin Luther, *Christian Liberty* (Philadelphia: Fortress Press, 1957), p. 7.

Metaphors of Freedom

The discussion of freedom with its need for boundaries may seem terribly vague to you. If this is the case, perhaps a few metaphors will help you visualize my idea of freedom.

Take the river, for example. It collects water from numerous tributaries until it becomes a large, flowing stream. The water flows between the banks that keep it channeled. So long as the water stays inside its boundaries, it provides beauty for an afternoon drive as well as a perfect place to go fishing and enjoy water sports. But when the river fills to overflowing, it floods the farmland, erodes the soil, and sometimes threatens whole communities. The river shows the importance of boundaries and the destructiveness of breaking through those boundaries. The river flows freely, yet it is bounded, and when it violates these boundaries, it loses its freedom and beauty.

A professional musician who has identified her gifts and uses them responsibly and fully provides another picture of freedom. A pianist, for example, who plays a Mozart concerto so immerses herself in the music that she becomes the music. From the standpoint of authorship, the music is not hers; it originated with another. Yet, in an existential sense, it is her music. She has studied it, internalized it, and now performs it with total freedom because it is hers. Freedom is the capacity to be grasped by and compelled by a power that enables you to be more fully who you are but manifests the creativity and genius of another.

Robert Shaw, a conductor who had long been retired, returned in the fall of 1998 to direct the Atlanta Symphony Orchestra in the performance of Bach's Mass in B minor. I was listening to the music when suddenly I noticed the conductor. His baton moved with precise strokes. From time to time he pointed to one section of the orchestra, then to another. At the proper moment he brought in the singers or the strings or the brass or the reeds. I saw a man lost in the music, and for a few moments he may have been the music.

Was Mr. Shaw operating from some sense of "oughtness"? Did he fulfill a command to direct the orchestra? No! No! Robert Shaw was doing what he wanted to do, using the gifts God had given him, and he was fulfilled through the experience. I suspect that God was also glorified.

Given how beautiful freedom can be, why do we so often fall into slavery? Did you ever see a buzzard float on the wind? If I had been reared in Alaska, I would describe an eagle, but since I grew up in southern Alabama, a buzzard is the best I can do. If you don't know about the buzzard, let me describe it for you: it is a large black bird with a wingspan of thirty inches or more. Among the birds, it fills the role of scavenger: it cleans up messes made by humans and other animals.

The buzzard doesn't eat living things, only things like dead squirrels and rabbits killed by an onrushing car or a crafty fox. This scavenger carries out its tasks at great risk because it works on busy highways and other places where it is vulnerable to foxes and raccoons.

The most notable talent of the buzzard is its ability to glide. When a buzzard is searching for the next clean-up, it flies aloft for a better view. After finding the proper altitude, the bird sits on the wind like a glider, barely moving its wings as it searches below for food. When the March winds blow, this old bird rides on the strength of the wind, and the harder it blows, the quieter become the buzzard's wings. It sits atop the wind and glides. Perhaps freedom is having the capacity to glide, even in gale-like winds.

Do these metaphors help clarify your vision of freedom? Freedom helps our lives to flow like a river, guided by the friendly banks. And freedom is the capacity to perform the work of another in a manner that demonstrates it is the work of both. Freedom is the experience of life that is constrained only by its deep desire and embraced sense of duty. Yes, the conductor does what he most deeply wishes to do, and, at the same time, it is what he ought to do. And the big bird doesn't fight the wind but extends its wings and rides on the breezes that blow. The Christian woman or man lives within the boundaries as a matter of choice. And the Christian so internalizes the grace of God that she does naturally what she ought to do. And, like a conductor, the Christian becomes the person who lives faithfully and lovingly. In seasons of stress the Christian rides the winds of trial. In all these ways the Christian experiences his or her freedom in Christ.

When we claim freedom in Christ, is it wishful thinking, or is it the reality of our relation with God? What does the Bible teach about this freedom?

Scripture Texts to Ponder

Then Jesus said to the Jews who had believed in him, "If you continue in my word, you are truly my disciples; and you will know the truth, and the truth will make you free." They answered him, "We are descendants of Abraham and have never been slaves to anyone. What do you mean by saying, 'You will be made free'?"

Jesus answered them, "Very truly, I tell you, everyone who commits sin is a slave to sin. The slave does not have a permanent place in the household; the son has a place there forever. So if the Son makes you free, you will be free indeed." (John 8:31-36)

Jesus promised freedom to those who follow him, and he made freedom contingent upon continuing to follow him. The freedom he taught emerges through the receptivity and response of us followers. Trusting Jesus as the Messiah as Peter did and walking away from the nets and boats is but the first step. Continuing to follow Jesus means learning the language he speaks and the response he desires.

In laying a foundation for living in freedom, Jesus rules out all social, cultural, and religious prescriptions. The Jews claimed they had never been in bondage; Abraham was their father, and he gave them freedom through the covenant. Jesus responded to their claim by pointing out that whoever commits sin is its slave, and the slave does not have a permanent place in the household of God.

Jesus concluded this discussion on freedom with an astounding promise: "So if the Son makes you free, you will be free indeed!" The Son by his death and resurrection liberates those who are in bondage to cultural demands and social norms so that they may live in freedom before God. This freedom includes freedom from all those forces that have invaded my life and yours — guilt, shame, fear, hypocrisy, greed, and the like. The freedom we seek comes from continuing to follow Jesus into a deeper knowledge of ourselves and a clearer vision of the world and our role in it.

As we walk this road, let us continually remind ourselves, "If the Son makes me free, I will be free indeed."

*   *   *

Paul's letter to the Galatian church addresses a congregation that had its original grounding in Jesus Christ and in him alone for its freedom. After Paul's sojourn with this congregation, teachers with a different message came to the city. They taught that Jesus was indeed the Messiah but that it was necessary for Christians to keep the Law of Moses, the Torah.

This demand offended Paul so deeply that he wrote a passionate letter to the congregation refuting the claim of the false teachers. Keeping laws can never set the slave free, he said. Freedom is the gift of Christ made possible through his death and resurrection. To look to anything other than Christ produces a false freedom. We can never achieve the freedom we long for through our own efforts. Paul will have none of this substitution of our performance for faith in Christ. Here is the heart of his argument with the false teachers about Christian freedom:

> For freedom Christ has set us free. Stand firm, therefore, and do not submit again to a yoke of slavery. Listen! I, Paul, am telling you that if you let yourselves be circumcised, Christ will be of no benefit to you. Once again I testify to every man who lets himself be circumcised that he is obliged to obey the entire law. You who want to be justified by the law have cut yourselves off from Christ; you have fallen away from grace. For through the Spirit, by faith, we eagerly wait for the hope of righteousness. For in Christ Jesus neither circumcision nor uncircumcision counts for anything; the only thing that counts is faith working through love. (Gal. 5:1-6)

"Faith working through love." This text illustrates quite clearly the freedom promised by Jesus. Jesus himself had said that his followers could not look to Abraham as the source of their freedom. Abraham was the titular head of the Jewish nation, the model of a faithful man, and one who trusted God. If the way of freedom does not flow from Abraham, where do we find it? Jesus was clear about the answer. He said, "I am the way, and the truth, and the life. No one comes to the Father except through me" (John 14:6).

Paul holds that Christ sets us free from rules and regulations. Christ sets us free from Moses' Law as a means of being made right with God. Specifically, Christ lifts the demand that all males be circumcised to prove they belong to God. Further, Paul argues that anyone who permits himself to be circumcised has cut himself off from Christ, has fallen from grace, and is obligated to keep the whole law.

Paul sees clearly two contrasting ways to live before God — trusting ourselves or trusting God. Trusting in ourselves includes trusting in our family name, relying on church membership or personal giving to the church, embracing noble causes, leaning on spiritual experiences, or depending on right faith or doctrine. Paul clearly rules out all these false liberators and every human invention we might look to for our freedom.

Christ and only Christ sets us free. He offers freedom as a gift. We receive the gift by faith in him. He, the Truly Righteous One, fulfilled all the demands of the law and therefore has the right to forgive and embrace us. The Great Apostle elaborates the positive aspects of this newly created freedom in Jesus when he writes,

> For the law of the Spirit of life in Christ Jesus has set you free from the law of sin and of death. For God has done what the law, weakened by the flesh, could not do: by sending his own Son in the likeness of sinful flesh, and to deal with sin, he condemned sin in the flesh, so that the just requirement of the law might be fulfilled in us, who walk not according to the flesh but according to the Spirit. (Rom. 8:2-4)

What does Paul mean by "the law of the Spirit of life in Christ Jesus"? I believe that Paul was trying to help Jewish readers see that Christ Jesus serves Christian faith like the Torah serves Jewish faith. The Torah embodies the will and purpose of God. When Israel abides by the revealed will of God, the Holy God is manifest in their actions. In a sense, the keeping of the law incarnates the Holy and issues in freedom for Israel.

Jesus' way of life consists not in a list of commandments but in a relationship through faith. When we turn to Christ in faith and receive him as Messiah and Lord, we turn away from ourselves as the source of freedom. As we live in obedience to Christ, he gives us the Spirit of life, the life-giving presence of God. He is the instructor and guide for our lives. So this inward presence guides and instructs Christians in becoming free and in using freedom. The Spirit of life within us empowers us to resist the passions of the flesh (old patterns, habits, and rationalizations developed through our efforts to set ourselves free) and to embrace the Spirit as liberated persons.

Perhaps no one delineates the works of the flesh more completely than Saint Peter. While Paul sets up the powerful contrast between the works of the flesh and the fruit of the Spirit, Peter shows the consequences of turning away from Christ as the source of freedom and points out what will happen to the unrighteous, "especially those who indulge their flesh in depraved lust, and who despise authority. Bold and willful, they are not afraid to slander the glorious ones" (2 Pet. 2:10). With an abundance of metaphors and allusions, Peter depicts the dire consequences for those who resist the Spirit:

> These people . . . are like irrational animals, mere creatures of instinct, born to be caught and killed. They slander what they do not understand, and when those creatures are destroyed, they also will be destroyed, suffering the penalty for doing wrong. They count it a pleasure to revel in the daytime. They are blots and blemishes, reveling in their dissipation while they feast with you. They have eyes full of adultery, insatiable for sin. They entice unsteady souls. They have hearts trained in greed. Accursed children! They have left the straight road and have gone astray, following the road of Balaam son of Bosor, who loved the wages of doing wrong, but was rebuked for his own transgression; a speechless donkey spoke with a human voice and restrained the prophet's madness. These are waterless springs and mists driven by a storm; for them the deepest darkness has been reserved. For they speak bombastic nonsense, and with licentious desires of the flesh they entice people who have just escaped from those who live in error. They promise them freedom, but they themselves are slaves of corruption; for people are slaves to whatever masters them. (2 Pet. 2:12-19)

Living before God in Freedom

What does the freedom of the followers of Christ look like from the inside? At the core of our freedom stands Jesus Christ, and his Spirit in us inspires faith in his adequacy. Christ alone guarantees our relation with God, and thus our freedom through his Spirit. To embrace anything else in addition to Christ shatters our freedom, and thus we must reject any additions to Christ if we are to be free.

What is freedom like in practical experience? To write about my experience of freedom feels risky to me. My fear does not arise from my resistance to being vulnerable; my fear is that you will read my witnessing as boasting. I hope you will read this witness as boasting in Jesus Christ; as Paul wrote, "Let the one who boasts, boast in the Lord" (1 Cor. 1:31). As I review my years as a disciple, I notice several basic changes that have come into my life and my relationships.

I no longer need to justify myself. I am made a just person in Jesus Christ. I am no longer condemned; sin has been overcome in Christ, and

I share in his victory. I do not mean that I am sinless — far from it. But I am forgiven and accepted in Christ.

The need to please others doesn't dominate my motives and thoughts like it once did. My growing concern is to live a life united with Christ through faith. Ultimately I hope to please the One who loves me unconditionally. I have begun to experience what it is like to be accepted by God without any conditions.

I know the freedom of accepting my body and not fighting with it constantly. Most of us, at one time or another, struggle with our bodies. We think we are somehow lacking in beauty — too thin or too heavy, nose too large or eyes too small, and on and on. We come to a sense of freedom when we embrace the person God made as well as the one we have formed.

I feel free to accept my gifts and not be jealous of those whose gifts are greater than my own. Like many young ministers, I had the dream of speaking to the multitudes, winning many persons to faith in Christ, and hearing the applause of my listeners. I suspect these yearnings were a mixture of youthful enthusiasm and my own ego demands.

After years of struggling with contaminated ambition (which never was fulfilled), I discovered that my destiny was not to address the multitudes but to help others discern their call and become equipped for their ministry, and offer support to them. After years of ministering in this fashion, I've come to see myself as a stagehand who pulls the curtains and affirms the actors for performances well done. In this way I have learned to fulfill God's will for me without wishing I could do what others are called and gifted to do.

I know what it means to desire the will of God even when I don't know God's will and am unsure of my ability to do it. Willing the will of God, no matter what it may mean, brings a simple, relaxed freedom. No one has written about this with greater clarity than Thomas Merton:

> My Lord God, I have no idea where I am going. I do not see the road ahead of me; I cannot know for certain where it will end. Nor do I really know myself, and the fact that I think that I am following your will does not mean that I am actually doing so. But I believe that the desire to please you does in fact please you. And I hope I have that desire in all that I am doing. I hope that I will never do anything apart from that desire. And I know that if I do this, you will lead me by the right road though I may know nothing about it. Therefore will I trust

125

you always. Though I may seem to be lost and in the shadow of death, I will not fear, for you are ever with me, and you will never leave me to face my perils alone.[2]

I know moments when God's will and my will seem to converge, and I experience a wholeness that issues in liberation. This convergence defines the freedom of being! As the Spirit transforms our inner life, and we truly desire the will of God, we cannot be overly burdened, oppressed by rules, or in bondage to anything or anyone. True freedom takes on a different meaning and feeling when we become aware that in some strange, mysterious way, we are united with God.

I make no claim upon God for this freedom in Christ. It is pure gift. By some work of righteousness, perversion of character, or ignoring of the Spirit, I can disrupt the peace that accompanies this freedom. Freedom, as I know it, is not a permanent possession. It is given from moment to moment and must be received and celebrated in the moment.

Celebrating Our Freedom

On the Saturday evening before Easter Sunday in 1998, I attended my married daughter's confirmation at the St. Andrew's Catholic Church. While waiting for the service to begin, I looked through the hymnal. My eyes fell on a section of hymns emphasizing freedom. The words of this hymn leaped into my mind and heart:

> When from bondage we are summoned,
>   Out of darkness into light,
> We must go in hope and patience,
>   Walk by faith and not by sight.
>
> When our God names us his people,
>   Then he leads us by the hand
> Through a lonely, barren desert,
>   To a great and glorious land.

2. This prayer comes from *Thoughts in Solitude,* though I'm not sure exactly where it's located in the volume. I found it on a small card placed in my room at the Monastery of the Holy Spirit.

At all stages of the journey
God is with us night and day,
With compassion for our weakness
Every step along the way.

Refrain: Let us throw off all that hinders,
Let us run the race to win!
Let us hasten to our home-land
And, rejoicing, enter in.[3]

Indeed, this is my prayer for you and for me.

Questions for Reflection and Discussion

1. What does it mean to be a free person? What is the difference between freedom and license?
2. Which of the metaphors of freedom best expresses the experience for you?
3. How do the Scripture texts cited define freedom?
4. Describe a time when you experienced being truly free.

A Journaling Exercise

1. List the things that keep you from being free.
2. Think of these as a person, an idol, a jailer, etc. Create a symbol for these enslaving things as a group.
3. Ask this symbol a question: "Why do I submit to you and lose my freedom?"
4. Write down what comes to your mind. You may wish to think about what they save you from, what they give you, and why you are reluctant to deal with them.

3. "When from Bondage," song no. 252 in *The Collegeville Hymnal,* ed. Edward J. McKenna (Collegeville, Minn.: Liturgical Press, 1990).

CHAPTER TEN

Remaining Faithful to the End

Living before God requires a tenacity, a stick-to-itiveness, a focus that refuses to be distracted by the lures of life on the outside or the clamoring voices of fear or pain on the inside. It seems no matter how old we are, forbidden desire stirs our passion, and the flawed assurance of perverted reason compromises our choices of the good in life. It would seem that age would diminish the attraction of forbidden fruit, or at least strengthen our will against disobedience. But instead, the urges become even subtler and catch our good intentions unawares.

So, after endeavoring to live before God for over a half century, I still have no place to let down my guard against those powers and principalities ever set to turn me away from the love of God. There is no safe haven into which I can sail, drop anchor, and rest on my accomplishments or degree of maturity.

In a powerful story called "The Monks' Distractions," Anthony de Mello illustrates in a concrete way the subtle temptations that keep us from living before God with unsullied dedication. He shows both the power and the persistence of temptation to turn us away from God:

> An urgent call came to the great Lama of the North from the Lama of the South. He asked for a wise and holy monk to initiate the novices into the spiritual life. The Lama of the North responded by sending five monks. Everyone was amazed and asked, "Why?" He answered cryptically, "We will be lucky if one of them gets there."
>
> The five had been on the road some days when a messenger ran up

129

to them. "The priest of our village has died. We need someone to take his place." The village seemed comfortable, and besides, they paid a good salary. One of the monks, seized with pastoral concern, said, "I would not be a good monk if I did not stay here and minister to these people." So he dropped out.

Some days later they happened to stay at the palace of a king who took a fancy to one of the monks. He said, "If you will stay with us, I will permit you to marry my daughter, and when I die, you can be king." What better way to serve the Lord than to rule the land? So he dropped out.

The rest of the group went on their way until one night, in a hilly region, they came upon a solitary hut occupied by a beautiful woman who offered them hospitality and thanked God for them. Her parents had been murdered by mountain bandits, and she was all alone and lived in terror. Next morning one of the monks said, "I will stay with her. I would not be faithful if I did not show compassion." So he dropped out.

The remaining two finally came to a village and found to their horror that all the villagers had forsaken the faith and were under the sway of a heretic. One of the monks said to the other, "I owe it to the Lord to stay here and to win these people back to the true faith." So he dropped out.

The fifth monk finally got to the Lama of the South.[1]

This story of the five monks concretizes the ways in which subtle and not-so-subtle temptations sway us from the commitment to live faithfully before God. Each monk had been chosen and commissioned by the Lama to train novices in the South. They left as a community of five to journey to their destination and accomplish their purpose, but they faced a series of distractions along the way.

The first distraction — to minister to a village without a priest — was a test to see if one of the monks would substitute a good thing for the best thing. Surely serving as a priest cannot be criticized, but the monk who agreed to do so had not been sent on this mission. By changing his focus, he allowed the good to rob him of the best. The monk whom the king fancied and who was promised a bride and a kingdom saw the possi-

1. Anthony de Mello, *The Song of the Bird* (Garden City, N.Y.: Image Books, 1984), pp. 82-83.

bility of doing great good through the wise use of power. When he compared the promised kingship with becoming a novice master, I wonder if he recognized the pride he would take in his new position? And did his repressed sexual desire unconsciously influence his decision? If these unacknowledged yet powerful influences functioned beneath the level of his awareness when he yielded to temptation, I wonder how they would manifest themselves when he ruled as king.

The monk who chose to remain behind with the beautiful woman terrified of living alone showed compassion. But was this pure compassion, or was it partly lust? This monk meant well, and his choice was expressive of his faith, but like the monk who received the king's daughter, he probably had mixed motives.

The fourth monk, powered by missionary zeal, dropped out of the journey to teach the truth to a village. Perhaps he reasoned that his instructing a whole village was more important than his forming a few novices. Indeed, the lure of this temptation, similar to that of the priest-less village, is religious fervor. Save the people from error! Yet this monk's zealous commitment and evangelistic passion turned him from his first calling.

In the end, one monk persevered to the end of the journey and served as the novice master for the aspiring monks of the South. Thus, the wisdom of the Lama of the North was validated.

If it takes five tries to get it right on our journey, it's too bad we have only one life.

The Wisdom of Jesus

The Lama of the North, knowing the frail character of his monks, sent five to accomplish the task of one. If, however, each of the monks had stopped to evaluate the journey, estimate the other demand being made, and consider the risks, would the result have been the same? Whether we begin this journey in obedience to a superior or with the enthusiasm of an adventurer, it behooves us to add up the costs. Jesus offers us this wisdom:

> For which of you, intending to build a tower, does not first sit down and estimate the cost, to see whether he has enough to complete it? Otherwise, when he has laid a foundation and is not able to finish, all who see it will begin to ridicule him, saying, "This fellow began to build and was not able to finish."

Or what king, going out to wage war against another king, will not sit down first and consider whether he is able with ten thousand to oppose the one who comes against him with twenty thousand? (Luke 14:28-31)

We have undertaken this journey of living before God not as an adventure for our adolescence nor as a support for our middle years nor even as a kind of security for our old age. We have set out to see it through clear to the end. This road of life, filled with changing scenes and abrupt, life-threatening challenges, calls us to make a complete trip. If we stop halfway, we won't make it home. If we turn aside after three-quarters of the journey, we still will not make it home. In the power of baptism, confirmation, and the Eucharist, we intend to go all the way.

Given the nature of the journey and its duration, isn't it wise to begin the journey by counting the cost? Must we not see if we have enough commitment to even begin the journey before we take to the road or go forth to do battle with the enemy? Wise persons who undertake this trek not only count the cost at the outset but also pause at each stage of life to count the cost of continuing the journey. If we turn aside before we arrive at home, those who observe will declare that we made a good start but were unable to finish the journey.

Today I find myself toward the end of my pilgrimage. I am not home yet, but I am much more than halfway, and I must still estimate the cost required to reach the goal. The face of retirement leering at me seems more like an enemy than a friend. One of the fearful aspects of retirement for me lurks in my sense of identity. For most of my life, my work has defined me. When I no longer am meaningfully engaged in my vocation or connected with a collegium, who will I be then? It's time for me to take stock, count the cost, and enlist soldiers of faith who can march with me.

Another self-revelation for me also lurks in retirement. I don't want to believe it, but at times I wonder if my love of God has been too strongly attached to my vocation. Have I, on too many occasions, reversed my priorities? Do I love God for God's sake? Or do I love God for my work's sake? The evidence suggests that when I am engaged in teaching or preaching or counseling, I pray seriously, with discipline, but that when I'm not serving in these ways, my prayer efforts slacken.

If my devotion to God is for the sake of ministry, what will it become when I am no longer hitched to the plow? Will my passion for God dry up? Will my head be turned in another direction? These thoughts

132

frighten me and force me to count the cost of being a disciple in the years beyond retirement.

On the other hand, as I move into the future, I recognize that this change could open up new possibilities for loving God — not for my work's sake or even for the sake of God's work, but for God's sake, for the sake of God's own self! Will this new frontier open vistas of grace I've never seen before, and will it beckon me into a future of undreamed-of possibilities? In this adventure of living before God, I discovered long ago that God does not tell us beforehand the secrets of our unfolding lives. We must live through the questions into the answers.

The Perseverance of Saint Paul

As I count the cost of ending my present vocation, the image of the runner who must run to the finish line to win the race gives me a model. In fact, Saint Paul uses this image to admonish us to remain faithful to the end. He says,

> Do you not know that in a race the runners all compete, but only one receives the prize? Run in such a way that you may win it. Athletes exercise self-control in all things; they do it to receive a perishable wreath, but we an imperishable one. So I do not run aimlessly, nor do I box as though beating the air; but I punish my body and enslave it, so that after proclaiming to others I myself should not be disqualified. (1 Cor. 9:24-27)

Saint Paul has his own version of faithfulness and perseverance. I have a hunch he would have given this admonition, plus his own testimony, to the five monks. He emphasizes competition, self-control, and self-denial to complete the race and win the prize.

If you think of the story of the five monks as the background for Paul's admonition, you get an idea why he calls for rigorous oversight of the body. Only one finished the journey, while the other four turned aside for a lesser good. Paul doesn't suggest that only one person will fulfill God's will; neither does he intend to stir up competition among Christians. Rather, Paul warns us against choosing the good instead of the best — that is, failing to fulfill God's will. At each stage of our lives we make choices, and those choices shape our direction and destiny for months

133

and even years to come. How important that we keep focused on the goal — living before God — and make choices accordingly.

The prize I seek today may be somewhat different from the one I sought earlier in my life. At one time I understood the prize to be eternal life or heaven, and certainly it is a prize! In another period of my life, my aim was to discern my identity and my gifts so that I could be fulfilled as a person. At still another period in my life, the prize seemed to be fulfilling my destiny through my work. Along the way I have occasionally fallen into the trap of seeking recognition and personal fulfillment as sufficient prizes. But now, as my journey draws closer to its end, I long to live my whole life before God. Heaven will take care of itself; fulfilling my destiny has been more or less achieved or lost forever; and personal recognition isn't worth commenting on.

I have no doubt that nearing the end of my journey creates this state of mind. Looking into the face of eternity sharpens my sense of the presence of God, the One who guides me in all of my choices. And I deeply want to live faithfully to the end.

Whether we focus on Paul's metaphor of a race or Jesus' emphasis on forethought in building a tower or going forth to do battle with principalities and powers, clearly these texts emphasize persistence to the end of the journey. Living before God is not only about beginning the race, digging the foundation, or responding to the struggle; it is about persevering.

How do we run this race so as to complete it? How do we press on without being distracted by the temptations of greed and the lust for power, as well as the temptations of the good and the compassionate so clearly displayed in the story of the five monks?

Wisdom for the Journey

I need wisdom to traverse this portion of the way, as I have needed it at every other significant portion along the way. I freely confess my need! But my need for wisdom now is not one wit less than it was at every step in the past. The end of life doesn't differ in quality from the beginning or the middle. Every unfolding stage of life has its challenges and its opportunities. For me, though, this final leg feels weightier than the other stretches because no time remains to recover from falls, poor decisions, or wrong turns. It's time to get it right.

If you came to me with the confession I am making to you and requested help, I'd give you the best wisdom I have. No matter what your stage in life, you face the same kind of issues that lie before me. In the first part of your life, you go to college, get a job, marry, and start a family. Every ten or fifteen years, the context of your life changes. You grow older; your job changes; your children grow up, leave home (and sometimes return home), get married, and have their own children — your grandchildren; and eventually you face the issues I'm facing: retirement and, at some point, death. Each stage has its own set of challenges, distractions, opportunities, and dangers.

It makes no difference which of these stages you are facing. You have never been at this place before; you do not know life beyond this particular crisis; the unexpected always comes to challenge your faith. Life is like that.

And if you asked me for wisdom, I would give you the best I know. If I would do this for you, why shouldn't I do the same for myself? So as I collect my own wisdom and write a few notes to myself, you may read over my shoulder to see if the wisdom offers guidance for you.

Keep Your Focus Clear

Keep clear your goal of living before God. You must run "where you are" on the course. Too many times you have restlessly assumed that God's presence was somewhere else. Try to remember that the time of Christ's coming is now, and the place of his action is here.

To journey where you are, pay attention to what's going on in your life. You have this capacity to notice. Who are the significant persons in your life? What demands are being placed upon you? How will you respond to your present challenges and opportunities?

To live creatively and passionately where you are, clear away the clutter in your life. You know what your clutter is. How do you spend your leisure time? What takes you away from the present moment? What do you use to occupy your attention when you could be engaged with Christ?

To live in the present, make friends with the inevitable and embrace the unchangeable.

Fight Important Battles

Not every issue is worth dying for. Choose the struggles that you have a chance of winning or making a difference in. Keep a balance between what you oppose and what you affirm. If your oppositions out-weigh your affirmations, you will become a negative, critical grouch. As you run this last leg of the journey, honor a few criteria:

1. Choose battles worth fighting. You will differ with others in the choices that you make. Choose the struggle that deserves your energy. Choose a battle that will make a difference ten years from now. Choose the engagement that is God's priority for you.

2. Choose the time for your fight. You can't always choose when to pick up arms because some battles are thrust upon you, but much of the time you can decide when to engage in a struggle. In your personal life there are seasons when you need to relax and rest. In your voca-tional life there are times when you need to keep focused on the task at hand. Stay engaged with the business at hand without becoming dis-tracted. Choose another time to deal with less pressing issues so that you do not neglect essential tasks.

3. Learn when to hold steady and when to relax, even retreat. When you're working for change, make your case, step back, and let the Spirit work. Remember that most of the decisions in our lives and ministries have some flexibility. Allow time and space for the Spirit to bring things to fulfillment. Don't consider your word or your vision to be final; it may be only part of a much larger picture that God is painting.

4. When you have suffered powerful blows from the Adversary and have been knocked down, get back on your feet. None of us wins every time. Defeat falls across every path in a variety of forms: failed intentions, unsuccessful efforts, and even wrong turns. These failures don't spell final defeat but provide an opportunity for you to learn the art of recovery so that you may continue on your journey. Re-member the testimony of Saint Paul to the Corinthian congregation:

> We do not want you to be unaware, brothers and sisters, of the affliction we experienced in Asia; for we were so utterly, unbearably crushed that we despaired of life itself. Indeed, we felt that we had received the sentence of death so that we would rely not on ourselves but on God who raises the dead. He who rescued us from so deadly a peril will continue to rescue us; on him we have set our hope that he will rescue us again, as you also join in helping us by your prayers, so that many will give thanks on our behalf for the blessing granted us through the prayers of many. (2 Cor. 1:8-11)

Keep in Shape to Run the Whole Race

If you intend to complete the race, keep your body and your passions under control. Temptations come from all corners. Discern the intention of God for you.

First of all, guard your sexuality. When you were a young man, you thought that age would diminish your interest in sex and in your ability to perform. Yet, when your ability becomes unpredictable, fantasy takes hold with greater frequency and persistence. You still can place yourself in compromising situations that will lead to your ruin and hinder the Kingdom of God.

You must pay special attention to the subtlety of these temptations today because of your fear of the loss of potency. Look at your brothers in the ministry. How many of them have failed at this one vulnerable point? Guard your mind and imagination. Keep your resolve to be faithful.

Also, beware of your use of alcohol. For many, it offers a temporary escape from stress and tension. An occasional beer or glass of wine is of no consequence, but when you allow one beer to become six and a glass of wine to become a bottle, you risk being enslaved or addicted.

If you intend to stay in shape for the journey, look at your calendar. For years your investment in work has been out of control. You have taught full-time, traveled almost every weekend, and written books sandwiched between those tasks. Who are you trying to impress? The administration? Maybe. The Lord? Perhaps. Yourself? Yes! Look at your calendar. Schedule a normal week. Rest. Play. Smell the flowers along the way.

For more than forty years you have battled your food addiction. Your body is crying out for relief from overeating. Now is the time for you to gain control of your eating habits. Choose today to seek comfort in your self-control, not in another bite of food, even the most tasty. Fill your emptiness with affirmation and God's delight, not with another dessert. Structure your life around the present moment, not around the next meal. Food is not a good substitute for God.

Handle money lightly. Don't become its slave. Once you struggled with the lack of money; now you think too much about money even though you have plenty to live on. Watch your lifestyle and don't become a slave to extravagance. Stand firmly against the enticements of this materialistic age.

Take special care that having adequate funds doesn't distract you from the goal. You have observed other Christian workers who inherited money or invested wisely and, due to their wealth, lost interest in God. Don't let this happen to you if your wealth increases.

In a sense, the last several paragraphs have been a paradigm of this whole book: reflections on the journey and things that I need to remember. But surely it has been more than reminders for me. Hopefully it has helped you to explore aspects of your life with God that you may have been aware of but never examined seriously.

At any rate, I have written about our continuous waking up to God, over and over again. In the process of waking up, it has been serendipitous to discover wonder — the prelude to faith, the first response to God, and the earliest form of prayer. Waking up and wondering are dual movements, with one evoking the other, and together they form a dance that escorts us into the presence of the Holy One. After more than fifty years of this dance, it has never gotten boring or monotonous for me, and it never will. How could dancing with the wonder of God ever be dull?

Life in the presence of God consists not only in dancing with awareness and wonder but in finding a solid footing in the Word of God. This Word that sustains the dance of mystery must never be reduced to dogma or a rigid morality, lest it lose its power to entice us into wonder. The Word is like a mirror that reflects the Lord; it also transmits the Spirit and shapes our lives. The Word is also like a solid foundation: without it, we would be dancing on a rotting floor unsupported by the sills of truth.

Living before God in this swirl of mystery that is grounded in the truth proceeds in spite of numerous deceptions. All our temptations are mere variations on a theme — "God cannot be trusted!" Whether it is turning stones into bread, leaping from a tower, or falling down to worship the Adversary, every temptation has at its core the mistrust of the Lord God. Those who live triumphantly place their trust in the steadfast love of the Lord, no matter what!

Hopefully we have begun to learn that living in awareness of the Other requires us to listen more than to speak. And listening introduces us to discernment — whose voice are we listening to? The voice of the tempter can be ever so subtle, and to discern who is speaking becomes an art.

Learning the art of living in the divine presence leads increasingly into living that way in smaller increments of time and space. With a bit of reflection and focused listening, we begin to develop the art of imagining the presence in an ordinary day. Encounters of the day that seem to be very ordinary, routine, and repetitious give us evidence of the Holy when placed under the microscope of faith. And every day — with its countless persons, gestures, experiences, and events — can be lived from one moment to the next. Each moment mediates the divine presence and becomes a sacrament filled with the Sacred.

Living before God resides not only in time, like the present moment, or space, like the day before us, but in our hearts. God is not only before us and behind us but also within us. The God who comes in time and space has now chosen to take up residence in our hearts, in the depths of our consciousness. Our great challenge, something we face every day of our lives, will always be to attend the God who both resides in us and is beyond us.

Living before God leads eventually into a glorious freedom. We live beyond the rules through a receptivity and ready response to divine love. What a joy to have our hearts attuned to the heart of God so that we do what we wish to do. Yes! We go forward in freedom, celebrating in joy!

Faithfulness is always about responsiveness in the moment and perseverance to the end. We have begun this journey, faced many crises, and now we are set to see it through to the end. Our eyes have become fastened on the Master of our lives.

A Closing Episode

As I was doing the final edit on this manuscript, I learned that a man I had been friends with for some thirty years had a tumor that was likely malignant. Before the final word was in, I knew the situation was serious. After hearing about the impending examination and possible surgery, I called on him.

On the way to his house, I recalled how I met Burney. He was a pastoral counselor in Athens, Georgia. I counseled with him for more than seven years, seeking to resolve my conflicted marriage. Now, as I drove toward his home, I thought about how he had helped me get well enough to see how sick both I and my marriage had been. He walked with me through the fear and pain of a divorce, and he has been there not only for me but for my children as well. To tell the whole thirty-year story would take far too long, but this much of it gives you a sense of this man's significance to me.

When I pulled into his driveway, Burney, his wife, and his son-in-law were deciding how to park three cars under a two-car shelter. He immediately invited me into the den, and his son-in-law gave me a glass of water. I began the conversation.

"I hear you've been in the hospital, Burney, and that's all that I know."

"Yes," he began, and then proceeded to tell me what the doctor had found. "Several weeks ago I had no energy, so I went to the doctor and began taking medication to correct that. I got no better, and about two weeks ago I began to turn yellow, so I went back to the doctor.

"They put me in the hospital and ran a number of tests. They discovered that I have a tumor on the pancreas, and it is likely malignant. Having examined the growth in relation to the blood vessels, they believe it is operable. Of course, they're not certain.

"So in four or five days I'll have the surgery. The physician has been very honest with me, as I had requested. He may open me up, find the tumor inoperable, and simply sew me back up. In that case, I have seven or eight months to live. Or he may be able to remove the tumor and treat the cancer, and after three or four months I may recover most of my strength.

"With respect to the surgery, the doctor explained that they rate the seriousness of surgeries from one to forty. This surgery ranks forty. My physician said, 'If my father, who is about your age, had this situation, I wouldn't operate; he couldn't survive the operation. But you have a much younger body than he does.'"

"How are you processing all this in your head, Burney?" I asked.

"You know how I am about these things, Ben. I'm not afraid to die because I don't look upon death as being the end but as opening the next stage for me. For years now I've been living my life in the present. I've never been promised more than one day at a time, and I've lived that way for a pretty long time.

"My faith has stood me in good stead. I have no fear. I'm not anxious. I hope the surgery goes well and that I have a few more years, but if they can't remove the tumor, I'm prepared for the next stage."

The conversation came to an end with my trying to tell Burney, in the presence of his wife, daughter, and son-in-law, what he had meant to me. I could never have become the person I am without his patient, sensitive counsel. My words were numerous but so inadequate.

Burney responded by telling me how much he loved me, how he appreciated what I had done for him, and that he celebrated the fact that God had used my life to bless scores of persons he couldn't name. For a long time he has been a surrogate father to me, and his words were the words my own father never spoke to me.

What did I see in the face of this man on his way to death? Faithfulness. He had done his homework in his soul. Long ago he had faced his own demons. Most he had conquered long ago. Knowing who he was and accepting his created being and worth, he did not strive for fleeting glory. I never met a man more at home with himself. He knew himself, felt at home with himself, and rested in this knowledge of truth. And it seems to me that the filter through which he saw God had been wiped clean of many of the smudges that blur the vision of so many. Living into the reality of life as it presents itself, he had learned to be faithful to himself, to God, and to all those who lived within his sphere of influence.

We prayed — or rather, I led us in prayer to the Father of us all. Our eyes bled tears as we sat together in hushed, holy moments. When I rose to leave, Burney followed me to the door. We hugged and said, "Good-by for the moment." As I drove away, I felt that Christ had mirrored himself to me in Burney. On the way home, I mused over the noble example of faithfulness I had observed in this man for more than thirty years. And now I was seeing that faithfulness hold him steady as he prepared himself for the next stage of living before God.

When the surgeon operated, there was nothing he could do. Burney was sent home to recover from the surgery and to die. Just a few weeks before Burney died, I visited with him, and in our conversation he spoke about the end of his life. "For me," he said, "this is the time to bring my life to an end. I have a number of things to wrap up before I finish this journey. At this time, for the most part it seems to me that I'm bringing the talents back to the Master, having used them faithfully and to the best of my ability. These gifts and capacities I have used all these years truly belong to Another. I return them with gratitude. Now I hear him saying, 'Well done, good and faithful servant. Enter into the joys of your Lord.'"

Could any of us ask for more?

Questions for Reflection and Discussion

1. What do the temptations of the five monks represent? Which one(s) do you relate to most?
2. What do Jesus and Paul teach about distractions in our lives?
3. What are the issues of faithfulness in your life today?
4. Where do you find help in dealing with these struggles?

A Journaling Exercise

1. List the things that seem to distract you from faithfully following Christ.
2. Write yourself a letter of wise counsel with respect to dealing with these.
3. Read over what you have written. Let yourself be surprised by the wisdom that you possess!

LaVergne, TN USA
11 November 2009
163801LV00010B/140/P